BLOSSOM

A BIOGRAPHY OF

MRS F.G. MILES

PUBLISHED BY
Cirrus Associates (S.W.),
Kington Magna,
Gillingham,
Dorset,
SP8 5EW UK.

ISBN 0 9515598 6 9

PRINTED IN ENGLAND BY:
The Book Factory,
35-37 Queensland Road,
London,
N7 7AH.

PHOTO SCANNING BY:
Castle Graphics Ltd.,
Nunney,
Nr. Frome,
Somerset,
BA11 4LW.

DISTRIBUTORS:
Cirrus Associates (S.W.),
Kington Magna,
Gillingham,
Dorset,
SP8 5EW.

COVER PHOTO: F.G. & Blossom Miles, Hugh Brooks and Charles Powis with the prototype Falcon G-ACTM (via Jean M. Fostekew)

ACKNOWLEDGEMENTS

The Author would like to thank the following for their help, advice, encouragement, and information:

Adwest Automotive plc, Peter Amos, Joan Angell, Nicola Beauman, P.A. Bentley, Gunter Bierman, David Broughton, Peter Campbell, Dave Chapman, Andrew Clark, Joan Cliff, Margery Cobby, Brian Cocks, Peter Davey, Patrick Davies, Kenneth Fostekew, David Godfrey, The Herald Society, Gordon and Yvonne Hessler, Mary Kearney, Cecilia Maude, Jeremy Miles, The Miles Collection, The Royal Berkshire Aviation Society, David Russell, Liz and Stuart Sarrailhe, Julian Temple, John Wakeford, all students of Miles Aeronautical Technical School and all the volunteers of the Museum of Berkshire Aviation at Woodley.

This book is dedicated to

ALL THE STUDENTS OF MILES AERONAUTICAL SCHOOL

1943–1949

CONTENTS

FORBES-ROBERTSON FAMILY TREE

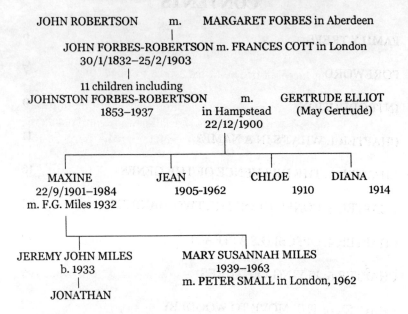

JOHN ROBERTSON   m.   MARGARET FORBES in Aberdeen

JOHN FORBES-ROBERTSON m. FRANCES COTT in London
30/1/1832–25/2/1903

11 children including
JOHNSTON FORBES-ROBERTSON   m.   GERTRUDE ELLIOT
1853–1937   in Hampstead   (May Gertrude)
22/12/1900

MAXINE   JEAN   CHLOE   DIANA
22/9/1901–1984   1905-1962   1910   1914
m. F.G. Miles 1932

JEREMY JOHN MILES   MARY SUSANNAH MILES
b. 1933   1939–1963
    m. PETER SMALL in London, 1962
JONATHAN

DERMOT/ELLIOT FAMILY TREE

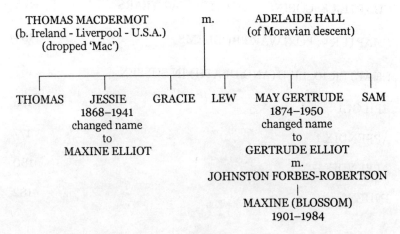

THOMAS MACDERMOT   m.   ADELAIDE HALL
(b. Ireland - Liverpool - U.S.A.)   (of Moravian descent)
(dropped 'Mac')

THOMAS   JESSIE   GRACIE   LEW   MAY GERTRUDE   SAM
1868–1941   1874–1950
changed name   changed name
to   to
MAXINE ELLIOT   GERTRUDE ELLIOT
m.
JOHNSTON FORBES-ROBERTSON

MAXINE (BLOSSOM)
1901–1984

FOREWORD

by

Peter Amos

(founder member of The Miles Aircraft Collection)

One afternoon recently I received a telephone call; nothing unusual about that, you may say, but this time the caller was Jean Fostekew. After the usual pleasantries had been exchanged the purpose for her call became immediately apparent.

"Would you be prepared to write the foreword to a book I have just written on Mrs Maxine 'Blossom' Miles?"

I was silent for a brief moment – an unusual enough occurrence for me – then I said: "Yes of course, I would be pleased to."

In fact I was honoured to be invited to undertake the assignment, but at the same time I was somewhat nonplussed because, although I have had more than a passing interest in Miles and his widely diverse range of aircraft since I was 17 years of age, I regret that I never worked for either Phillips & Powis or Miles Aircraft. My interest was first aroused when on Sunday, 20th July 1947, while cycling around the home counties aerodromes, I 'stumbled across' the last Miles Aircraft Open Day which was in progress at Woodley.

I went on to spend the best part of a lifetime in the aircraft industry but I have always maintained the greatest admiration for the pioneering work of both the Miles brothers, F.G. and George, and F.G.'s wife Maxine (or 'Blossom' as she preferred to be known).

It was left to Don Brown, Miles' lifelong friend and cohort, to sum up the wonderful relationship of the Miles family, in his book *"Miles Aircraft since 1925"*:

> "The practical but impetuous Miles with his tremendous energy, enthusiasm, force of character and drive; George with his clear, logical and incisive mind, while sharing his brother's flair for design and mechanical ingenuity and Blossom, clear-thinking, calm and well balanced – a perfect counterpart to her impulsive husband and shy brother-in-law."

Now, at last, the fascinating story of Blossom Miles has been told, and by another lady, who in my opinion is the one best qualified to tell it.

7

Jean was one of the early students of the Miles Aircraft Technical School, established in 1943, and as such came to know Blossom very well. In producing this most interesting insight into her background Jean has filled a very important gap in our knowledge of a most outstanding lady.

It has been my pleasure to have known Jean since the early days of the Berkshire Aviation Group, which has since become the Royal Berkshire Aviation Society and from which the original idea for the Museum of Berkshire Aviation stemmed. Jean was one of the founder members of this museum, in which she is now deeply involved in a voluntary capacity, and she is also a member of The Miles Aircraft Collection, of which I am proud to be the honorary general secretary. It is one of the aims of The Miles Aircraft Collection to ensure that the good name of Miles and all that was achieved by it in its 15 years at Woodley, in the very forefront of British aircraft design and production, is not forgotten.

Although much has been written on Miles and 'his' aircraft over the years, too little credit has been given to Blossom, his most able wife, and I am now very pleased to see that the balance has at last been redressed. I commend this book, not only to the aviation historian, but also to all those interested in the role of women in education, the arts and industry.

INTRODUCTION

There are women aviators who are household names and whose biographies have been written many times over, but there is one woman in aviation who deserves this recognition who hitherto has remained largely undocumented.

She was born Maxine Forbes-Robertson but was known in the world of aircraft and aircraft production as Blossom Miles.

Unlike most of the other famous aviatrixes, she was not only a pilot but a designer, draughtswoman, aerodynamicist and stress engineer, a director of a manufacturing company which at one time employed more than seven thousand people. And there are still more attributes: she brought up a family, was a caring and brilliant hostess, designed theatrical costumes, edited journals, wrote articles, promoted health and housing issues, collected the literati and doyens of the artistic world around her, took in refugees from all over the world and found them jobs. She was artistically gifted herself and encouraged others to their full potential. Her lasting and enduring legacy was to her students. The painstaking and time-consuming effort she readily devoted to the Miles Aeronautical Technical School has paid dividends, not only for the students themselves but in the wider aspect of world aviation. One of her students has written from Provence fifty years later that: "she was a wonderful woman in all respects, just so much personality and . . . an engineer too."

Later in the text you will read that she writes in one of her articles that: "I cannot go on in the third person." Her biographer has that problem as well. Being so closely involved with the tale about to unfold, this biographer cannot help but resort to the first person occasionally, while desperately trying to sound objective. Therefore "I" will briefly sketch my own interest in this project. In 1947 I was fortunate to be accepted for a place at the Miles Aeronautical Technical School (M.A.T.S.) at Woodley Airfield near Reading (known as Reading Aerodrome for much of its existence). Blossom Miles was the main inspiration for this school, as stated before, and therefore I was influenced greatly not only by the education but by her attitudes to life.

I went on to work in the aircraft industry – Flight Development at Fairey Aviation and the Air Survey Company. I then lived in the U.S.A. and other locations. By chance, many years later, I became chairman of the Museum of Berkshire Aviation. Having previously taken on the task of tracing the old students of M.A.T.S. and sending newsletters and arranging reunions (although reunions had been arranged in the 1970s, unbeknown to me at the time), I heard the words so many times and from so many different mouths that "someone should write a biography of Blossom"; so while waiting a few years for that "someone" to turn up I embarked on this book while there are still some of us sufficiently *compos mentis* to have enough recall and retrieval in our systems. Thus I hope that the reader will understand and forgive the syntax.

CHAPTER 1

WHAT'S IN A NAME?

She was christened Maxine Frances Mary Forbes-Robertson, when she married she became The Honorable Mrs Inigo Freeman-Thomas the Viscountess Ratendone, and then . . . she fell in love with someone called Fred.

Was it a relief, I wonder, after the trauma and scandal had died down, as it always does, to be able to sign her name for the rest of her life "M. Miles"?

This slim, elegant, artistic daughter of a famous theatrical family possessed talents in the fields of all the arts and languages; she also had personal magnetism, a great zest for friendship and education and for forming and developing societies of all kinds. At the same time she held the skills which were to be the ones which made her famous, those of learning to fly an aircraft in a then record short time, being able to design aircraft both technically and artistically *and* become a director of an aircraft company which would hold national and international records and world-wide acclaim.

This polymath was to achieve the highest triumphs – she was the first woman to be appointed Commissioner of the Civil Air Guard – but she was also to suffer bitter personal tragedies.

Women in aviation have always been rare. *"Rara avis"* is more than apt. Even in the nineties there are just a handful of women flying airliners in British Airways. In the past women pilots were so rare that they became household names all over the world – after Amy Johnson and Amelia Earheart, how many others immediately spring to mind?

Of course there are very important women aviators, but so few compared with men, and unless they did something dramatic like Amelia Earhart and disappear without trace they won't be remembered by any but the aviation buffs and a few historians.

Blossom Miles was different from those like Jacqueline Cochran, Harriet Quimby, Jean Batten, Lettice Curtis, Sheila Scott, Beryl Markham, Hanna Reitsch and the Duchess of Bedford (and she *did* disappear without trace) in the fact that she virtually founded an empire of beautifully designed efficient aircraft and developed educational and training establishments with a far-seeing, *avant garde* inspiration in tandem with flying aircraft, lecturing and writing, and bearing and bringing up two children.

All this time, she had only one eye.

*   *   *

Much of this book is based on personal memories of those who knew her and, as such, may not be entirely accurate. Personal memories are invariably selective, including my own (*especially* my own); therefore I must apologise in advance for any inaccuracies or emphases that may not entirely concur with the memories of those of us who are still alive who knew her. Subjectivity is a problem none of us can escape; so what follows is unashamedly subjective.

As far as my own recollections go, well, I can think of nothing negative. As Blossom's student I remember her in a golden light. I never heard a bad word of her or saw any dissension amongst her contemporaries. I never heard any negative comments or criticism of any kind. Maybe this makes a one-sided, even boring picture of her, but I can't help that: I only knew, saw, and heard good of her. Perhaps this is not possible of any human being . . . but there it is.

If this makes her sound like a saint, well, no, she could hardly have been called a saint, having had an illicit love affair, smoking like a chimney and driving her car like a maniac; just a warm vulnerable woman like many others and yet not quite like the rest of us.

Posterity plays strange tricks. It is said that everyone is famous for fifteen minutes, but the Miles family, Blossom, F.G. and George Miles were famous for at least fifteen years. Yet today there are very few not intimately connected with aviation who remember them and their products.

However one name connected with them on several counts is still famous, and that is the name of Sir Douglas Bader. The first question that school children ask on entering the Museum of Berkshire Aviation at Woodley is almost inevitably about Sir

Douglas because they all know that that is precisely where he had the tragedy to lose both his legs. The fact that this was in 1931 before the Miles family had come to Woodley is just one quirk of fate in the line of events which was to lead to Douglas owning and flying Miles aircraft both during and after the second World War. The Miles Master he said "was without vice" and the Miles Gemini he flew in later years was a familiar sight in the sky at White Waltham airfield in Berkshire. One of the last photographs of Sir Douglas before his death was taken in the board room of Adwest Engineering at Woodley, probably the very same room which had been the board room of Miles Aircraft.

Sir Douglas Bader's fame lives on, deservedly so. This book tries to redress the obscurity into which Blossom Miles and her husband are rapidly disappearing.

Although the scientific theory of chaos had not been propounded when Blossom started her career in the aircraft industry, she would have been interested to tabulate how many random events had to take place for her future to be determined. If a certain little aircraft had not crashed into a ditch at Shoreham in 1930, if Fred Miles had not landed at Woodley to refuel on a flight back from Gloucestershire, if Dr Csato had not made her acquaintance, if . . . if . . . if. Maybe even if she had not been nicknamed "Blossom," or not lost an eye, would she have risen to such great heights?

Adversity seems to be a great motivator: should we have heard of Douglas Bader if he had not lost his legs? Would Sydney Camm have designed the Hurricane had he not been brought up one of twelve children in a tiny terraced house? The examples are legion.

But one does not readily associate adversity or disadvantage with Blossom. To all intents she would appear to have been born with the proverbial silver spoon in her mouth, and there is no doubt that the high profile of her early life influenced her later social life, her aspirations, and the way she was to cope with officialdom, commerce and the political implications of running a factory with many diverse departments and all their requirements, a factory that was to employ as many as seven thousand workers at the height of its operations.

All the gifts that Blossom brought to the partnership with Fred Miles and the business that grew out of that partnership were complemented in an equal and opposite sense by the genius that Fred had been incubating before they met.

In the strange way that fate seems to intervene in the lives of the famous, and those who are to become famous, these two, when they met, must have recognised the chemistry which was to cement the attraction, both physical and psychological.

At the risk of sounding like a cheap romantic novel, they were probably powerless to deny their love and the strength of it.

That they were total opposites in many ways will be shown graphically in the following chapters, and especially in literary articles they both wrote, sometimes in the same journals; and yet their love and marriage endured until Fred's death at the age of 73.

To return to the theme of the name paradigm at the beginning of this book: Fred was known through most of his business life and by most of his colleagues as "F.G." This makes one wonder if this was a subtle variation of a class-conscious or class-difference problem which could not quite come to terms with the name Fred.

Interestingly enough, this is borne out by the fact that when Fred and Blossom were first 'a couple,' Fred was known by her friends as simply "Miles," which obviously could just as well have been a Christian name as a surname and had a certain upper-class quality about it as a forename.

"Frederick" itself is a noble enough name, and although of Teutonic derivation actually means "peace ruler"; this was not quite appropriate perhaps for F.G., or it may have simply rather fallen out of fashion at that time in the century.

The name "Maxine" might betray the fact that her mother was an American; the nickname "Blossom" (although 'nick' hardly seems the right prefix to use for such a beautiful name as Blossom) may owe its origin to being based on the Old English "Blostura" – one who is lovely and full of promise.

Full of promise she certainly was, and lovely with it.

We will see in the next chapter that "Maxine" was an entirely made-up name, and we will discover the reason for her being thus named and also the probable reasons for Maxine being discarded in favour of Blossom.

Readers might wish that all the characters in this book maintained the same name throughout its action. Unfortunately all our main protagonists had at least two different soubriquets – and in several cases three – during the span of this volume.

CHAPTER 2

THE INFLUENCE OF THE GENES

Well, how can we explain Blossom's talents?

We really need to go back no further than her paternal grandfather to see how she might have inherited the genes to make her a polymath.

However we shall go back at least one generation before her grandfather because this is where the Forbes came to be linked up with the Robertson, and perhaps this was the critical combination that resulted in so many talented members of one family emerging.

The fashion for combining the mother's surname with the father's to form the now much maligned 'double-barrelled' pseudo-aristocracy crystallised at about the right time for the Forbes to be linked with the Robertson. Both were obviously good old Scottish names and we must guess that both branches were proud of their names and antecedents. That they had cause to be proud of them, we can only surmise with the evidence before us. However we have to start somewhere and so we shall start there.

Genealogists must be grateful to this fashion of hyphenation as it has in many cases made their lives and their research so much easier. Forbes seems to be a name more often hyphenated than most others. It has been joined to a great many others; examples spring to mind, Forbes-White, Forbes-Harris, Forbes-Wake etc. Although Forbes would appear to be a fairly common name and therefore one might assume that there would have been a need to separate it from the throng, it is not actually such a common name as, say, Ford, for instance, which is hardly ever joined to another to distinguish it.

Forbes-Robertson – it scans well, impressive but not too fancy or fanciful, it has a good ring to it, it has all the makings of a good omen and, for several generations, it appeared in successive volumes of *"Who's Who"* and was a well-known, almost a household, name. It has only in recent times disappeared from

16

"Who's Who," and strangely, about the time it vanished, that was the edition when the surname of Fred Miles started to feature in *"Who's Who."*

Blossom's paternal great-grandfather, John Robertson, married Margaret Forbes of Aberdeen in the early part of the nineteenth century and thus founded a family, a dynasty one might say, which was to become a household name in that century and the next, famous for more than one reason.

They had a son, an only son, John, and that is when the names were linked; this was Blossom's grandfather. John Forbes-Robertson was born on January 30th 1822. He showed extreme academic talents from his youth. Luckily his parents could afford to give him an excellent education and he attended Grammar School, Marischal College and the University of Aberdeen. Nevertheless some of his education was down to his own efforts and brilliance because he held a bursary by a scholarship competition while at University. He was a prize-holder in more than one class and, while still a student, he was on the literary staff of the *"Aberdeen Herald"* and the *"Aberdeen Constitutional."*

Aged just 21 years he came down to London, where he studied further at University College. It seems incredible at such a young age and at that time in the century, but he then travelled to the United States of America, where he studied for a season; he then came back and went to continental Europe, where he visited all the principal art centres of the European countries.

Eventually he settled in London and adopted literature as his profession. In the present age it is hard to imagine that that bald statement was enough to provide him with both a reputation and money sufficient to live on, but evidently this was so because he wrote several books that we know about and possibly many more that it is difficult to trace now. We know that he wrote *"The Great Painters of Christendom," "The Life of Gustave Doré," "The Life of Rosa Bonheur"* and lives of other artists.

We also know that he was art critic on *"The Art Journal"* and *"The Magazine of Art,"* and art critic on several other weekly publications, prestigious London ones as well as provincial magazines which, no doubt, provided income if he needed it. We don't really know if he was living on the income from such sources or not, but it looks very much as if he did, otherwise why should such an erudite art authority bother to write for out-of-town journals? Perhaps this need to make money followed the family throughout several generations. On the other hand his address in London was 22 Bedford Square, definitely not a downmarket situation. It was obviously a family home because his son also had that address throughout most of his life.

22 Bedford Square was a beautiful, very large house (it had five flights of stairs) designed by Adam, and it still exists today, adorned by a commemorative plaque. Blossom was to love this house.

John Forbes-Robertson's clubs were given as Aberdeen University, London and Aberdeen, still close to his Scottish roots. His "recreations" were extremely worthy and altruistic. *"Who's Who"* in the edition of the end of the 1800s lists his recreations as being:

"Guardians' *(if you have ever read Charles Dickens'* "Little Dorrit" *you will realise what a devoted and charitable person he must have been)*, 'Member of the Central London Sick Asylum' and 'President of the Commissions of the Free Library of St. Giles and St. George's, Bloomsbury.'"

All of the above give more than a clue to what must have been an almost saintly disposition and how that was passed down to his grandaughter.

His appearance, too, must have been imposing: he had a great black beard and a strong Scottish accent.

He married Frances Cott in 1850 in London, and in 1853 his son named Johnston, who was to be Blossom's father, was born. They had eleven children altogether, six boys and five girls, eight of whom were still alive in 1925. Frances was endowed with the finely-cut, slim facial features that Johnston inherited, as did Blossom and her son Jeremy. John Forbes-Robertson remained famous enough to be included in *"Who's Who"* from about 1867 until well into the 1900s.

But in 1891 blindness prevented any further work and this quality unfortunately was also to be handed down to his grandaughter. He was totally blind by the time his son Johnston was married in 1900. He used to run his hands over his pretty daughter-in-law's face to try to picture her features; this she found rather disconcerting at the time.

He died on 25th February 1903, so that we can assume that by then he had known his baby granddaughter Maxine, who had been born just over a year before; even if he had not actually been able to see her physically, we can hope that he held her. She was living at the same address for a while after her birth, although that event did not actually take place at Bedford Square; but shortly after her birth the elder Forbes-Robertsons, John and Frances, were moved out of 22 Bedford Square to a house nearby – the rather contentious reasons for this will be covered in a later chapter. Thus it is possible and even very likely that the old grandfather held the tiny Blossom in his arms.

The name Forbes-Robertson apparently was not of sufficient status to appear in *"Who's Who"* between 1916 and 1928 and then in the 1929 edition we find "Sir Johnston Forbes-Robertson."

We wonder at the compiler's reasoning because Johnston Forbes-Robertson was created a Knight in 1913, so obviously recognition of his talents and importance was already well under way by the end of the nineteenth century. Perhaps that fact reflected the rather lower esteem in which the theatre was held compared with the world of literary and art journalism at that time of Victorian standards and prejudice; naturally this is only a guess based on historical data.

The kudos which an entry in *"Who's Who"* underlined and the snobbery surrounding it was rather contradicted by the fact that Johnston appeared in the 1911 edition of *"Encyclopaedia Britannica"* and this was *before* he was knighted.

Johnston, born in 1853, was described as "the eldest son." He was born in London at 22 Bedford Square, where he lived most of his life. Students of numerology might like to read something into this stable '22' and also of his future telephone number of 'Museum 1212' (a similar number was to become a household word).

Like his father, his education was exemplary, as he had attended Charterhouse and Rouen. France was also to play a large part in his daughters' educations. He then studied at the Royal Academy of Arts because he intended to become a painter. He maintained his interest in the visual arts and obviously had been talented enough in that field to have been accepted by the Royal Academy in the first place. However he turned from painting to the theatre. He was an actor from the age of twenty-one. Once again we marvel at so much education and experience being obtained in such a short span of lifetime.

He did say that he was unable to make a living out of painting, so had to turn to acting to earn enough money. However examples of his work show him to be a very competent artist, even one of genius, and a photograph of him at the age of seventeen shows him dressed as a character in a play, so he appears to have been bitten by the acting bug early in life.

He was a pupil of Samuel Phelps, who taught him the tradition of the tragic stage as it was appreciated at that time. His first appearance on the professional stage was in London as Chastelard in *"Mary Queen of Scots."* He was such a success that he became a leading actor at Bancroft's and Hare's Theatre. His outstandingly good looks and lean, athletic figure made him an ideal leading man and photographs of the period show him looking incredibly like his daughter Blossom.

He acted with the Bancrofts ("Sir Squire Bancroft" was held in such awe) and with John Hare, all very famous theatrical personalities then, and is described as "supporting" Miss Mary Anderson both in England and in the United States of America. Like his father he was willing to go far afield in that era of notorious discomfort as far as long-distance travel was concerned.

In their book, a very weighty tome in at least two large volumes called *"Mr and Mrs Bancroft on and off the Stage"* they refer to Johnston playing Count Orloff in *"Diplomacy"* in the 1877-8 season, but perhaps more interesting in our context they say that an admirable portrait of the famous actor (by this they mean Samuel Phelps) in the character of Cardinal Wolsey was painted by Johnson Forbes-Robertson who "like Jefferson combines the use of his palette and maulstick with his love for the sock and buskin"; they also remark that Johnston often played with the old actor Phelps at the end of his career.

This portrait was, by the subscription of a hundred of the members of the Garrick Club, purchased by the Garrick and "added to the valuable collection of paintings owned by the club."

We probably know of the use of the "palette and maulstick," referring to Johnston's talent and love for the visual arts, but we might wonder what the "sock and buskin" mean. As these terms are quite archaic, the reader may be wishing to know that the Bancrofts meant comedy and tragedy, as the "sock" was a a type of half-stocking worn evidently only by actors in comedies, although originally it meant a low-heeled shoe also worn by comic actors; whereas "buskin" was a high-heeled half-boot which evidently was worn only by actors in tragedies, usually with the toes poking out. The conventions of the theatre seemed to be quite rigid, and it must have been quite a comfort for the audience to have a sort of code to help them interpret the action!

A little later, in the 1883-4 theatrical season, another aspect of Johnston's talents which was to become a feature of Blossom's accomplishment, that of costume design, was mentioned by the Bancrofts:

> "The gavotte we introduced in the 'Tea-Room' leading from the pump-room where hung the authenticated portrait of the city's former king, Beau Nash, was the result of some pains, and the designs for the historically correct and beautiful dresses were made by Mr Forbes-Robertson."

Blossom was to show many aspects of her interest and involvement in the theatre, especially many years later when she sponsored and encouraged the pupils at her aeronautical school to form a dramatic society and provided them with a competent and experienced coach. She also gave them the facilities to screen avant-garde and foreign films at a time just after the second World War when these were an extremely eclectic and esoteric interest. Pupils thus received a wider education and a broader view of life, having these opportunities at the school in the evenings and on half-day holidays.

Even today Sir Henry Irving is remembered, and Johnston acted with him on more than one occasion, when Johnston's "refined and artistic style" and his beautiful voice and impeccable elocution made him a "marked man," to quote a contemporary account on the English Stage.

In 1889 at the Garrick Theatre he played the major role in *"The Profligate"* by Pinero, under the management of John Hare. This role, more than any other, led to the establishment of his reputation and his position as one of the most original, talented and individual of all the London actors of that period.

Blossom, therefore, her genes waiting in the wings, was programmed from long before she was born to become uniquely special in whatever field she would eventually choose to devote her talents.

Her father became an influential theatre manager in 1896, when presumably his youthful appearance must have been beginning to fade, but strangely he did not marry until 1900 when he would have been 47 years old.

He actually started under his own management in 1895 at the Lyceum. Apparently he must have been in partnership with the famous Mrs Patrick Campbell, beloved of George Bernard Shaw, because they produced "Romeo and Juliet," "Hamlet," and "Macbeth," which may seem to modern-day thought as being singularly unimaginative and playing safe with the repertoire; but he also produced "some modern plays," the identities of which seems to have been lost in the mists of the end of the century. Nevertheless his Hamlet was described as being particularly fine and his capacity as a romantic actor was evidently still well to the forefront in spite of encroaching middle-age, because the reviews he got at that time for his role in John Davidson's "For the Crown" and in Maeterlink's "Pelleas and Melisande" brought superlatives from the critics.

May Gertrude Elliot was an actress who used the name Gertrude Elliot on the stage and in 1900 Johnston married her.

Gertrude Elliot was an American, the daughter of Thomas Dermot of Oakland, California. She was actually born in Rockland, Maine, but her father moved to California after the death of her mother. The difference in the surnames will be unravelled later. However she was a beautiful leading and talented actress and was Johnston's leading lady in many productions.

How many times in recent history has the combination of American and British genes produced offspring of genius? We need only to think of the Churchills, the Astors and a multitude in the arts and theatre. Gertrude and Johnston appeared together in many productions, among them "The Light That Failed" and Madeleine

Lucette Riley's *"Mice and Men"* (this was years before Steinbeck, was a real tear-jerker and had the audiences sobbing loudly), George Bernard Shaw's *"Caesar and Cleopatra"* and Jerome K. Jerome's oddly-titled *"Passing of the Third Floor Back."*

Shaw actually wrote the part of Caesar for Johnston Forbes-Robertson, so great was his reputation and power of his performances.

Gertrude continued to act even after the death of her husband. In John Gielgud's memoir *"An Actor and His Time"* he describes "Lady Forbes-Robertson, the widow of the great Sir Johnston" as being on tour with him in America in 1936. He may be slightly in error as to the exact date, or he may have been writing in retrospect as Sir Johnston did not die until later.

They had four daughters, of whom Blossom was the eldest. Jean Forbes-Robertson was to become a noted and excellent actress in her own right. The use of the word 'talented' becomes exceedingly overworked in the context of this family. Johnston also had three brothers and a nephew in the theatre. Two of his brothers we know about; they chose not to retain the hyphenated form and strangely one chose Robertson as a surname and one chose Forbes. Perhaps this was not so strange if they already had an older brother with the name Forbes-Robertson working in the theatre, but nevertheless they were quite well-known to their generation.

Ian Robertson was born in 1858, Norman Forbes a year later in 1859, and they were both famous actors from about 1878 onwards. Their father must have wondered why his sons should choose such a precarious profession, but it seems that they all made a success of their careers, although he was not to live long enough to see his eldest son knighted in spite of living to be eighty-one.

Evidently Sir Johnston looked outrageously theatrical when he walked about London. He effected an elegant frock coat and a top hat with a curly brim long after this mode of dress had ceased to be fashionable. His facial features retained their handsome, high-cheek-boned ascetic demeanour into old age and his sheer presence was overwhelming.

Johnston's talents were not entirely confined to the theatre and painting – far from it; like his father and at least one of his daughters, he was something of a polymath. He held an Honorary

Master of Arts from Columbia University U.S.A. and an Honorary Doctorate of Literature from Aberdeen University. He wrote a book in 1925 (when he was seventy-two) entitled *"A Player Under Three Reigns"* and his recreations were listed as "painting and gold." His clubs reflect his status: The Athenaeum, The Beefsteak, The Garrick.

His farewell tour as far as the theatre was concerned commenced at the Drury Lane Theatre in 1913; at the age of sixty he must have felt it appropriate. He lived to be eighty-five years old, his father having lived to eighty-one – his daughter Blossom was to live to eighty-two.

His daughter, Jean, was not so fortunate; she died at only fifty-seven, but more of her life will be revealed later. Sister Chloe died even younger.

It must seem strange that Johnston did not marry until he was forty-seven years old, but what turned out to be a very happy marriage to a girl less than half his age at the time of their wedding came about because of the following circumstances. As a young actor of considerable good looks and talents he first fell under the charms of the famous Ellen Terry. There is no doubt that he loved her and indeed was in love with her. She was by far and away the best-known actress of her generation and also of generations to come. However she preferred the attentions of Sir Henry Irving who, of course, was also the most famous male actor, perhaps of all time.

It was a typical coming together of the giants of the stage which has happened so many times since, and, whether for business reasons, or sexual, or both, Ellen Terry became what was called "the special property of Henry Irving." Johnston Forbes-Robertson then withdrew from the contest; this may have been because he held Irving in such high esteem, which he did, or because of many other reasons hidden in the mists of time.

He next fell in love with Mary Anderson. She was an American actress, beautiful, we are told, a blonde of a certain amount of talent, charms and intellect, and a devout Catholic. They were actually formally engaged to be married.

Now the Forbes-Robertson family had been brought up in a very different manner from the vast majority of Victorian families. They were what was known as 'free-thinkers,' extremely strict and ethical, but nevertheless with marked objections to rigid religious doctrines and their practices. Johnston paid homage to the philosophies of William Morris and John Ruskin, and categorically refused to have any of his possible future children brought up as Roman Catholics; this brought a strain on the relationship that just could not be resolved, so this engagement was broken and another romance 'bit the dust.'

His next love affair and romance was so destructive that it was a wonder he survived, and he very nearly didn't. Mrs Patrick Campbell (her Christian name was Stella), was famous, or notorious, for her relationship with George Bernard Shaw, well-documented in their published letters.

Johnston, as his daughter Diana, said, "had the misfortune" to fall in love with Mrs Patrick Campbell. As they were closely involved professionally both in acting and managing, it was difficult for him to break away from her influence.

She was temperamentally like an active volcano. We must wonder if in actual fact she hated men. Once she knew that a man was in love with her (and many were), she held them in her power with such vitriolic schemes and diabolic tortures, not only in private but on the stage as well. She taunted Shaw with Johnston and Johnston with Shaw. She played tricks on Johnston during performances to put him off his stroke, she devised stunts to make him look a fool, and because he loved her he put up with this treatment until in the end it made him extremely ill indeed.

We wonder how any woman could behave like this and still hold men in thrall. To quote Diana again:

"Mrs Patrick Campbell had fluid grace, a fascinating mobile face, lambent eyes, tip-tilted nose, and a lovely young body she dared to use."

In 1899 Johnston was so ill that he had to leave the stage (some thought for ever) and, protected by his brothers, Norman Forbes and Ian Robertson, fled to the continent. Now an uncle of Patrick Campbell, who had been killed in the Boer War, presented himself at 22 Bedford Square demanding that Johnston should marry Stella because he had compromised her and the family. At that time Johnston was in Sicily so he was saved from an even worse fate.

However his mother Frances was more than a match for the uncle and told him a few home truths about the precious Stella.

This episode says a lot about Blossom's father. It tells us that, although he had a very successful career, the admiration of the critics, his audiences, his family and indeed the general public, he was very vulnerable even at the age of forty-six to emotional turmoil. This sensitivity and his caring, finely-tuned feelings must have made him an ideal father, even though he came to that role very late in life.

What about Blossom's mother? Up to now she has seemed a shadowy figure, very much in the background, very much in the 'supporting role' both in the theatre and in home life.

It is surprising to find that her ancestry and upbringing is just as notable in its own way as her husband's. "In its own way" – that is the crucial phrase. Different as the proverbial chalk and cheese were Johnston and Gertrude, in very much the same way as Blossom and Fred were to be.

Names are just as important in this part of the story but in a totally different context. The various changes that names, both Christian and surname, undergo during the telling of this tale are both confusing and frustrating to the reader and biographer alike.

Let us go back to the potato famine in Ireland. In the early 1800s a small boy called Thomas MacDermot, his mother having died of starvation and having no home, made his way somehow to Liverpool, but there he found things not much better. At the age of twelve or so he was one of the so-called Liverpool 'dock-rats.' That is, he lived by his wits on the dockside. He lived in an old hogshead, which had originally held molasses but which he lined with straw or paper. The boys fought over anything they could find, any scraps of discarded food from the ships were enough motivation for a bloody fist-fight.

Whilst one of these fights was in progress, a boat from America docked and the wife of the Captain took it upon herself to intervene with her umbrella. All the other boys fled from her wrath and the religious homilies that were being delivered at them based on her Methodist convictions. One boy, however, did not run away, whether in the hope of money, food or a pat on the head from a kind lady; kindness was not an everyday sentiment there.

Captain and Mrs Ames (as this lady proved to be) had lost several children of their own in infancy and early childhood only recently, and fate had intervened in a way that she was sure the Good Methodist Lord had intended. Like a plot of one of the romantic plays in which his daughter was later to gain success, the story unfolded; the boy Tom was taken on as a cabin boy on the return voyage and taken to the Ames' home in Rockland, Maine.

When they got to America, the Ames decided that Tom must drop the 'Mac' from his surname, because there was so much prejudice against the Irish immigrants at that time, although later to be of Irish ancestry was quite an advantage in the States. Funnily enough, the MacDermots with one 't' were considered to be of a more upmarket lineage than those with two 't's. Tom's eldest daughter was to marry a MacDermott with two 't's as her first husband, and she was to have several more changes of names, not only surnames but Christian names as well.

Tom Dermot prospered in Rockland and became a master mariner and eventually a sea captain and reasonably wealthy. He married a Rockland girl, Adelaide Hall. She was a studious, serious girl whose mother, a Moravian, had come from Bohemia because her family considered that the Protestant religion in that country had become too wishy-washy and folk needed a stern code of ethics to live by. She was very beautiful but her upbringing had implanted the seeds of a propensity for serious depressive illnesses which, coupled with constant migraines, eventually led to her being confined in a lunatic asylum and her early death.

Before this happened, however, Tom and Adelaide had had six children. The eldest was a boy, Thomas, melancholic like his mother; then Jessie, who was to change her name to Maxine and become the most famous of the family; then Gracie, who died in infancy; then Lew, who became a seaman and died at sea quite young; then May Gertrude, born on December 14th 1874 (she was to become Blossom's mother); and then finally Sam.

May Gertrude lived in the shadow of her older sister. They were very close emotionally and Jessie looked after May Gertrude to such an extent that she arranged for her to follow a theatrical career simply so she could keep an eye on her throughout her own travels as an established actress.

Now Blossom was christened 'Maxine' after her aunt; therefore we must pay attention to her aunt's life as it had such an impact on Blossom, on her father, mother and the whole social life of that time at the turn of the century and for the next twenty years.

Maxine Elliot was described as the most beautiful woman in the world. King Edward VII was one of many who said so, and he was something of an expert on feminine beauty. Fashions change so it is difficult to judge from photographs, but evidently her eyes were something quite out of the ordinary and could actually change colour with her emotions. She certainly had a following amongst her audiences that amounted to adoration. She was so famous on both sides of the Atlantic that it hard to believe that she is unknown today. Nevertheless we have all heard of her name, Maxine.

This was a name she entirely invented. It did not exist before she thought it up, and as her niece Diana said: "All the girls named Maxine to the present day have her to thank" (or otherwise) for that name. I think many of us would remember that one of the Andrews Sisters was called Maxine.

Her name, as we know, was Jessie Dermot; not a very exciting sound to it, she thought. Her nieces called her Aunt Dettie, a far cry from the glamorous creature that she was. When graduating from tuition in the acting profession, her mentor, Dion Boucicault, suggested that she think of the most impressive name she knew. She replied that the most important-sounding name she could imagine was a man's name, Maximilius, the name of the father of one of her school friends. They played around with variations of Maximilia and so on through Maxime to, finally, Maxine – and so it was.

How much this name contributed to her success is only conjecture, but possibly quite a lot; and so the seeds were sown which would result in her acting career, in her sister Gertrude's acting career, in their success in both America and England, in Gertrude meeting a fellow actor, which in turn would result in the birth of her niece Maxine, and the fact that this name would be hated so much by her future brother-in-law, Johnston Forbes-Robertson, that his daughter Maxine would forever be known as Blossom.

Maxine discarded her surname Dermot as well. Elliot happened to be a Christian name of a branch of her mother's family and found favour with her advisors, and so Maxine Elliot rose from an inauspicious beginning into being one of the most famous names in the world.

There is no doubt that she had a very hard early life; the fact that her father was so typically stern and strict with his children and, no doubt, unsympathetic and irritable to his wife who was ailing both mentally and physically, meant that she bore all of the stress and burden of being virtually the head of the little family. The characteristics that she developed as a teenager were both the making of her and the undoing of her. This, coupled with her striking appearance and courage and determination were to influence not only her contemporaries but, in the future, Blossom as well.

Her beauty, apart from being her main asset, was also a curse. There were rumours that she had had an illegitimate pregnancy when only fourteen years old, but this is not proven. Certainly her first marriage to George MacDermott was a complete disaster. Her second marriage, to comedian and actor Nat Goodwin, was not much better, but by then she had learnt to make the best of any situation and to control her own finances.

There was a closeness between the two sisters that was the result of the difficulties they experienced with regard to their mother. Mrs Adelaide Hall Dermot was a sensitive, quiet, withdrawn woman, very beautiful but delicate and suffering greatly from migraine attacks. Her husband, Captain Tom, was a hearty vigorous type who liked a drink and was severe and harsh with his children. Gradually Adelaide's condition deteriorated into a zombie-like terror. She would take the younger child May Gertrude, when only six or seven years old, out in the streets at night and walk about in the dark. Meanwhile the elder sister Jessie was left to run wild and look for love and affection elsewhere. Jessie also had to shoulder most of the responsibilities of running the household as her mother was increasingly unable to tackle the tasks and her father was often at sea.

Consequently Jessie looked on May Gertrude as her responsibility and almost as her own child, and Gertrude grew up deferring to her sister and trusting her judgement. When she became Maxine this relationship was even deeper. Maxine was to have no children of her own and her care of and power over Gertrude became almost obsessive.

Having cajoled and bribed her own way into the theatre business, Maxine then set about doing the same for her sister. She changed her sister's name from May Gertrude Dermot to Gertrude Elliot; she wanted to make sure that no one was under any illusion that Gertrude was given parts only because of the vast influence of Maxine. She saw to it that the younger girl had only ingenue and supporting roles; she was perfectly sure that Gertrude's quiet, shy type of prettiness and her pliable nature would never outshine the great star qualities and spectacular beauty of Maxine. By having the same surname she had greater control over her sister and sent the message to the world at the same time.

It was a terrible bombshell to Maxine when Gertrude married Johnston Forbes-Robertson.

It so happened that one time when Maxine had to go back to America to fulfill a role she was contracted to do, just then Gertrude had been awarded a part in a play in London. Maxine thought that Gertrude was being chaperoned so tightly that Johnston, or any other man, would never be able to be alone with her, but love found a way.

Gertrude wrote to Maxine telling her that she was engaged to be married to Johnston. Maxine wrote back saying that she absolutely forbade it. This shows exactly how she saw her relationship with her younger sister, even though Gertrude was in her twenties. She wrote that Johnston was far too old for her (at forty-seven, this was quite true) but she also wrote that Gertrude was far too young: at twenty-five this was hardly true. Maxine wrote disparagingly of life in the theatre, the drudgery of it and the uncertainty, and telling Gertrude to marry a rich man, preferably a Lord with a mediaeval castle, so that Maxine could have a great time "improving the bathrooms."

All this was too late. Gertrude, with uncharacteristic determination and fingernails bitten down to the quick in nervous anticipation of her sister's wrath, married Johnston on December

22nd 1900. In Cincinnatti Maxine would speak to no one and spent a miserable Christmas alone.

Meanwhile, after a hilarious wedding where the parson forgot *his* lines, attended by most of Johnston's ten brothers and sisters and his mother and father, so many of his relations insisted on signing the register as witnesses that the certificate looks a mess with so many signatures, those of Norman Forbes-Robertson, Francis Forbes-Robertson, Ida Buchanan (his sister), Ian Robertson (his brother), John Forbes-Robertson (his father), Madeleine Lucette Ryley and H.B. Harrod (whoever he or she may have been). They were married by licence at All Souls Church in Hampstead. Both of them were described as "players." Johnston's residence was named as 22 Bedford Square and Gertrude's as 35 Clifton Hill which is between South Hampstead underground station and Maida Vale. Johnston's father is described as a journalist and Gertrude's as a Sea Captain. Gertrude was given away by the actor John H. Ryley (whose wife was the playwright Madeleine Lucette Ryley) and from the Ryley's house they set off for a honeymoon in Biarritz.

This was so successful that Gertrude found herself pregnant in the first month of marriage. This fact was to enrage Maxine even more but she managed to get her own back on Johnston, something for which he never forgave her.

It happened like this: Maxine had a magnificent house called "Jackwood" built at Shooters Hill on the outskirts of London; she was determined that her sister and her new husband should come and live there with her whenever she was in England. Johnston resisted all her efforts to get him under her power in this way and he was determined to continue living at 22 Bedford Square, where both his parents still lived and there was plenty of room for him and however many of his siblings wanted to stay at any one time. His sisters, especially, were running in and out of the place all the time.

He was a polite, considerate man, not wishing to make trouble for anyone, particularly his new wife, so there was an armed truce between him and his sister-in-law. On the surface, everything was amicable.

In 1901 Maxine was going to open in a play in England with her husband Nat. They were due to play at the Comedy Theatre in *"When We Were Twenty-One"* in September, not long before Gertrude's baby was due.

Also in that September Johnston was committed to resume a tour, mainly in Scotland; certainly he had to play *"Hamlet"* in Glasgow. Anyway he went off, not too worried about Gertrude, as she had a little more time before she was due to give birth and he was completely happy with all the arrangements that had already been made at 22 Bedford Square. The best doctor had been engaged, nurses also, and all preparations made for her room, linen and accoutrements. Of course, the senior Mrs Forbes-Robertson had had eleven pregnancies of her own and come through them all safely, if slightly disgruntled, so everything that *could* be done *had* been done; and so Johnston went off to Scotland with an easy mind, although wishing that he did not have to go. Maxine, with the coast clear, had other ideas. She preyed on Gertrude's susceptibilities by saying that 22 Bedford Square was too gloomy, too depressive, its aura was all wrong for bringing a baby into the world, the old man was blind and fumbled about, the old woman was sad and bitter and that there were Forbes-Robertsons of all shapes and sizes infesting the place, including sister Daisy who was a dwarf.

Gertrude was not used to defying her sister and so, on September 20th, although her time was very close, she allowed herself to be taken to Jackwood by Maxine, just for the day she thought. The weather was glorious and Gertrude certainly felt her spirits lift in the lovely surroundings of Jackwood. She took Maxine's two dogs for a walk, but they got extremely muddy, and Gertrude, with her worried nature, fretted over them getting Maxine's beautiful carpets dirty, so she decided to give them a bath. The whole effort and physical strain of this operation brought on her labour and nothing, just nothing and nobody was prepared for this. The local doctor could not be found, so someone went dashing to look for a midwife. Constance Collier, the English actress, was staying at Jackwood and she described the panic and frenzy of activity which went on, but she herself could do nothing more than follow Maxine and Gertrude and make things worse by being in floods of tears.

Maxine's husband Nat, though not good for much usually, seemed to know about hot water and towels; the old American pioneer spirit surfaced and he calmed things down, but Gertrude was in the very final moments of labour before the midwife arrived, and she and Nat Goodwin together delivered the baby girl who was to be named Maxine and always called Blossom.

CHAPTER 3

CONFLICT OF THE TWO MAXINES

There used to be a saying in the aircraft industry: "If it looks right, it *is* right."

This tenet might be more difficult to defend in these days of advanced military and transport aircraft, which could be described as incredibly ugly as the availability of highly efficient powerplants has transcended aerodynamic considerations; but even the uninitiated would probably admit that Concorde or the American Stealth bomber does indeed "look right," and, in fact, looks beautiful in an artistic sense.

When Blossom designed aircraft, her signature was indelible; later Miles aircraft not designed by her are so obvious that they stick out like the proverbial 'sore thumb.' This is not to say that they were any the less worthy or valuable, having been designed to a specification or for experimental purposes, but her designs were so artistic and beautiful that their lines never go out of fashion.

Now designing aircraft is not just a matter of art: a great deal of mathematics is involved, physics as well, of course, and an all-round grasp of the sciences. From the previous chapter we can understand her artistic skills, but where did all that specialized mathematics come from?

Strangely enough, there are more hard facts and data about her sister Jean's education that can ever be unearthed about Blossom's, but we might well assume that Blossom's education followed a similar pattern. Jean was the next daughter born on the 16th March 1905, just about three-and-a-half years younger than Blossom. Jean Forbes-Robertson was educated at "Folkestone, Ascot and France." We also know that her youngest sister Diana, known as Dinah, went to Heathfield school.

Whatever the actual content of Blossom's education, it was obviously intended to be wide-ranging and to equip her for what was considered a suitable entry into society in the early part of the

34

twentieth century, but one cannot help thinking that in those days mathematics would not have had a high profile. However when we consider Blossom's early artistic work we find that there were certain elements about it that had a definite mathematical, engineering and practical slant. She is described as a competent engraver, a woodcut artist, even a gardener.

Of course, even before her education began there were other influences. Her heredity we have already discussed. Her birth to a comparatively elderly father, his first and eldest child, would likely have meant that she would have been thought of, and treated, as a very special daughter; this might have given her a degree of self-confidence which she was certainly going to need in later life.

Now the loss of her eye at an early age must have influenced her and affected how she was handled and managed, so that this handicap may have been pressure both in a positive as well as a negative manner. She may have had a privileged position because of it as well as what most of us would consider a very great disadvantage.

Evidently the loss of her eye was the result of a severe reaction to the vaccination against smallpox. Inoculation against the small-pox virus was compulsory in Great Britain between 1843 and 1948. In the earlier years a larger amount of vaccine was used and this sometimes resulted in very bad reactions and even death in some infants. It seems a hard price to pay, but of course the programme did result in smallpox being eradicated worldwide by 1980.

Babies had to be vaccinated within a certain time of birth and only if the parents had any religious or other hardened objections to the procedure could they get a dispensation against the injections. This had to be applied for judicially and the result was that parents in a humbler position than the Forbes-Robertsons would have had to take a day off work, which most of them could ill afford to do; consequently smallpox was eliminated from Britain much earlier than from many other countries.

Most people who knew Blossom in later life might have been unaware that she had a glass eye, so little did she make of the handicap; being used to it from an early age, she took it in her stride. Her youngest sister Dinah always thought that Blossom had been born without the eye; it seems to have been a subject regarded as sensitive and not discussed even within the family. Her son Jeremy said that she would not smoke a cigarette whilst she was driving a car because, being conscious of needing full vision, she was careful not to risk smoke getting in her eye. This is one of the only times I have heard of it affecting her behaviour.

Most of the photographs of Blossom seem to be profiles; even the one of her with her three sisters taken in about 1914, although beautifully posed and showing the very different characteristics of the four girls, shows her profile only and with her eye tightly shut. If this photograph is printed the right way round (and this is something one can never be sure of, especially in old reproductions) then it shows her left eye closed. Most photographs show that her right eye appears to be the glass one, but there are several portraits of her with eyes closed. One often notices that a glass eye can look more real than the seeing eye, thus confusing the onlooker, who is usually under a certain amount of embarrassment when meeting someone with this sort of handicap and afraid of being thought to be 'staring.' There is a rare full-face photograph of her taken in 1935 with Charles Powis and F.G. which shows her smiling but with a strained expression.

*   *   *

Well, we have seen how and when she was born. We don't know how much she weighed but we do know what happened when her father came down from Scotland expecting to be back in plenty of time for the birth. He rushed to 22 Bedford Square where he knew all preparations were in place to be met by silence only broken by his mother who, no doubt expecting some sort of fireworks from him, said first of all: "Everything is all right."

Poor Gertrude in the latter stages of her first pregnancy could hardly be expected to make a measured judgement or to stand up against her sister's forceful and experienced cajolery, but giving in to her sister's quite reasonable arguments at the time really did affect Blossom's life and development in the short and long term.

The sumptuous decor and furnishings of Jackwood, too, played their part in the merry dance of life, of Blossom's life. The ultimate luxury in which Maxine lived, and in which she did for all the rest of her life, is difficult to account for merely in terms of "good investments." Money is not supposed to bring happiness but it did to Maxine – where it came from is another matter.

To return to Johnston: there could hardly be two more different personalities than Johnston and Maxine, the twin influences on Blossom. Did they complement each other?

Now Johnston, or "Forbie" as his sister-in-law always called him, was a gentleman, but he was also a gentle man; however he was ready to forget both meanings of the words when his mother said those words: "All is well" in a voice trembling with disappointment or fear, or both.

Johnston had caught the night train from Edinburgh to London and felt supreme unease all through the journey, although the baby was not theoretically due right away. On that same train was Alexander MacKenzie, then a well-known composer; he nobly tried to take Johnston's mind off his stress by recounting tales of musical mishaps and so on, but Johnston could not concentrate and was so relieved when the train reached London that he could not quite take it in at first that the bedroom so carefully prepared for Gertrude was empty. His mother told him that Gertrude "had been obliged (*'obliged'* he thought!) to go to stay with her sister at Jackwood."

Maxine had had her way, and worse was to come.

His frame of mind is illustrated by the fact that he said, after his dash to Jackwood at Shooters Hill that there he was *"allowed* to hold my first-born in my arms."

There was evidently no question of moving the new mother, so the carriage was sent to Bedford Square to collect all the baby clothes and other essentials. Johnston was forced to leave again early on Monday morning because he had to play Hamlet in Glasgow. The train was late and the play had to be delayed until he arrived, so he was doubly upset and angry.

He did admit to his brother Ian who was also playing in Glasgow that he agreed with his comment: "Well, I suppose you'll tell me it's the most wonderful infant you've ever seen."

Of course, by then Maxine had the upper hand in managing her sister and her new niece, and her strong personality did continue to influence Blossom and the way she was brought up for a great deal of the girl's youth, and possibly all her life.

Although Johnston was deeply resentful of Maxine's influence and was so for the rest of his life, and – as stated before – never forgave her, he still gave in to her on another point, and for this he never forgave *himself*.

This was because Maxine considered that life in Bedford Square was not suitable for Gertrude because of the presence of Johnston's parents, and kept delaying the return of the mother and baby under this pretext. Gertrude in her post-natal phase was no real judge of the situation and Johnston had to be away so much that, in the end, under all this pressure he agreed to move his elderly parents out of this house they had lived in so long, and found them rooms in another house as close by as he could.

The sad fact that neither of them survived more than a few months after this upheaval need not necessarily have been solely caused by the move; nevertheless it appeared to Johnston that he had signed his parents' death warrants by giving in to Maxine. Actually his father was away in Scotland when his mother died and when he got back to his rooms, he just faded away.

Thus we have Blossom's early years with many hurdles to overcome, and she was an only child for nearly four years (until her sister Jean was born in the late spring of 1905), an only child of an elderly father racked by guilt and a mother torn between her dominant sister and her gifted husband.

By the time Blossom was two years old she was in America. Maxine and her husband, Nat Goodwin, had to return to the United States in January 1902 to tour. Maxine was remote and the marriage was totally unsatisfactory for her. Whether she managed to arrange it or whether it was just a coincidence, in 1903 the Forbes-Robertson family were booked to open in a play in New York, *"The Light that Failed"* by Rudyard Kipling. They took Blossom with them and first of all went to the opening of Maxine's latest play in Buffalo.

Blossom, barely two years old, seemed to find an affinity with her uncle, Nat Goodwin. Perhaps there was some indefinable link because he had attended at her birth, or just the fact that Nat, for all his drinking and womanising, was a warm, good-hearted, fun-loving character and, as such, enjoyable for a little child to be with.

Nat once said to Constance Collier that he had "married the wrong sister," but surely Gertrude could not have coped with him any more than Maxine could. Many years later he was about to marry his sixth wife just as he, inconveniently, died.

Blossom and her sisters' births were well spread out for those days when families were resigned to having a child at least every two years or sooner. The fact that Johnston was forty-eight by the time Blossom was born may have had something to do with it, or the fact that Gertrude was involved in the theatre as well as her husband might have made too many pregnancies a matter of conflict with schedules. Certainly they both appeared fertile enough for Gertrude to have conceived in the first month of marriage. Blossom having been born in 1901, Jean was not born until 1905 (this was another thing that Maxine was *most* cross about), then Chloe was born in 1909 and Diana not until 1914 when Johnston would have been sixty-one.

Apart from the American tour, it doesn't seem that Blossom was toted around the theatres too much. She had a devoted nurse, "Nonny" (otherwise Miss E.M. Biller), who didn't think too highly of Aunt Dettie (as Maxine was known to the girls). One of her famous roles was in the play "Her Own Way," her own title for it, I believe, and she was seen romping with children much to the audience's delight. Nonny snorted loudly during this scene as she never 'romped' with her nieces but only wanted them dressed up to the nines as an accessory to her own fashionable appearance. Blossom, being the eldest, came in for a great deal of this fussing and preening and hated it.

*   *   *

The interest and excitement of aviation at the beginning of the twentieth century affected everyone, rich and poor alike. It was, after all, something entirely new. Although future developments could only be imagined, still the possibilities of flying through the air filled the whole country with awe and anticipation. Jules Verne, with incredible powers of prophecy, had set the scene long before, and now, it seemed, the most far-fetched of his stories was about to come true.

Blossom, even as a child, shared in the general intoxicating curiosity, but she had influences closer to home with regard to flying.

George Bernard Shaw, who was one of the close coterie of the Forbes-Robertson theatrical circle, wrote a play *"Mesalliance"* as early as 1909 in which the whole crux of the plot revolves around an aircraft crashing into the greenhouse of the characters who have, so far, appeared in the play; but further to this there is actually a *woman* in the 'plane who, although not flying it, is instrumental in saving the life of the pilot and totally reorganising and affecting the lives of the rest of the cast. This woman is pivotal, and we are given to believe that she could have piloted the 'plane had she so wished. Now all this was written and performed such a short time after the first manned flight of the Wright brothers.

There is a photograph of Claude Graham-White landing his aeroplane on Blossom's aunt's lawn, whilst her aunt's butler and house guests look on. It may even be Aunt Maxine in the cockpit (well, hardly a cockpit) with Claude. Graham-White is described by the Forbes-Robertson family as being a rather rough man with no social manners, but actually he came from a wealthy family and could afford to indulge his passion for aviation. He could easily have been the first man to fly across the English Channel instead of Louis Blériot, because he went to France to buy the Blériot machine, which happened to catch fire in the air while Blériot was demonstrating it to Claude. It was totally destroyed but Blériot obviously survived somehow. This didn't seem to put him off, but it meant that Graham-White had to wait while another aircraft was produced for him and, I think, in the meantime Louis Blériot made history.

Although Claude Graham-White did set up manufacturing aircraft in his own name, the one in the picture looks like a Farman, probably the MF-7 Longhorn. This, in spite of its primitive appearance, was used in the first World War as a training aircraft and an observation platform. This was designed in 1913, so Blossom could only have been twelve or so when she came in contact with this accessary to her aunt's social scene.

Another aviation influence was Lady Kathleen Drogheda who was a very early and daring aviatrix and a close friend of the family.

She was the wife of the Earl of Drogheda of the Foreign Office. She was described as "headstrong," and entertained Blossom with tales of delightful flights, but she was also willing to get down and scrub the floor when it became necessary during the war. Her giddy manner concealed a real talent for organisation.

Blossom may have known that Wiley Post, who flew around the world not once but twice, and the second time solo, had also lost an eye in a drilling accident and overcame the handicap to become so famous in the world of flying, but that was to come later in 1931.

In the meantime, Blossom's childhood was spent among the rich and famous. There is a photograph of her and her sister Jean, aged about eleven and seven respectively, hand-in-hand with the Duke of Rutland and looking most miserable about it. When her father presented her to Lord Curzon he recited the honours and offices of the Lord to her. Lord Curzon replied: "Perfectly correct, perfectly correct." It must have been a daunting life for a little girl and probably rather boring too. She may have started dreaming about the freedom of flying in the sky then.

*   *   *

Blossom was the only one of the sisters who had a clear recollection of life before the first World War, and she was very conscious of how that changed not only her own life but everyone else's too. But if life before the war had been hamstrung by protocol and etiquette, and if she hoped for more informality afterwards, she was disappointed because her Aunt Maxine took over her niece's life with even more determination and zest.

However there was still the conflict between the artistic circle of her father's friends and the fashionable Lords and Ladies and social climbers of her aunt's coterie. Each set contained some very famous personages.

Her aunt's followers had more influence on Blossom because she spent more time with them. Her mother was a pliant little soul, involved with the theatre more and more and also, of course, with the younger children, as well as being under the dual influences of both her sister and Johnston, as Blossom was. Johnston was often away; he and Gertrude did manage a short holiday in Switzerland for the Christmas of 1906 but we don't know if they took Blossom and Jean with them or not. But in 1915 a tour in the States involved him in playing in 122 towns in six months. How he ever kept up such a high standard as he was noted for amidst all that travelling, dressing, costume changes and learning his lines is hard to contemplate.

Blossom, like Gertrude, longed to please Maxine, but somehow neither of them really managed to achieve it. Maxine was inordinately pleased when Johnston got his knighthood in 1913. This made her sister a "Lady."

Johnston said to Blossom: "Your aunt dearly loves a title."

He was known to let out a loud theatrical "ha!" when Maxine said to Jean that: "A Lord is just that much better than anyone else."

Johnston, Sir Johnston, "Forbie" to Maxine was "Dad" or "Dadsy" to the four girls; this illustrates his essential modesty under all his theatrical and social success.

Johnston's friends included such talented and famous people as Walter Sickert, Alma Tadema, Swinburne, Max Beerbohm and Jerome K. Jerome as well as all the famous stage personalities and, of course, George Bernard Shaw and Sir James Barrie. Tennyson, Whistler and Wilde were also known to him but they died just before Blossom could have met them.

In contrast, Maxine's acquaintances read very differently: King Edward VII, Prince Francis of Teck, Lord Rosebury, the Duchess of Sutherland, Sir Winston Churchill, Lord Sandwich, Lady Carnarvon, Baroness d'Erlanger, hardly anyone who wasn't at least "an honourable." So perhaps it was inevitable that Blossom should meet and marry the son of a Viscount.

Before that happened, however, Blossom endured a great many clothes fittings under the expert eye of her aunt. Once she had to stand for so long while hems and frills and bits and seams were tacked and adjusted that she fainted. Maxine did show a little concern then – she said: "Don't tell your mother."

Even after all this striving for perfection, Blossom was always very disappointed because, for all her wealth, her aunt was obsessed with making over second-hand clothes to fit her niece, who longed for something new of her own. Maxine liked to have power over her poor little dressmakers as well as over her niece and sister.

When Maxine came to reopen Hartsbourne after the war, Blossom remarked on how changed she was. Maxine had never got over the death of Tony Wilding, and the facial resemblance later of Fred Miles to one of the photographs of Wilding was significant in the fact that before the war Blossom also adored him as a child. It was not just that she followed her aunt in her affections but he spent hours patiently coaching the little girl in tennis and bending down over her to adjust her racquet grip; they made a pretty and sentimental picture. He won the men's singles title at Wimbledon in 1910, 1911, 1912 and 1913. When he was beaten for the first time in 1914 tears rolled down Maxine's cheeks and her whole body was shaken with great sobs as he lost point after point to Norman Brookes who was his friend and doubles partner. Brookes was so surprised to win that he too was emotional and his racquet "shook like a butterfly" and he won the final point on a mis-hit off the wood. Maxine's friends including Lady Drogheda were shocked and upset. Tony Wilding was the only person on the court to maintain a calm, cheerful aspect as he put his arm round Norman's shoulders and laughed his way off the court.

Tony Wilding was not just a great tennis player and he was certainly not a gigolo although so much younger than Maxine. He was prepared to do any hard work, no matter how dirty it made him, or odd jobs like mending cars and helping anyone who needed it, without a thought of how it might upset his schedule or mealtimes.

After he was killed by a shell which landed in his dug-out while he was sleeping, Gertrude said: "Oh! what a dear Tony was," and Johnston said: "Tony Wilding was a great gentleman."

So therefore a great gloom descended upon Maxine and her house, which she sought to sublimate by house-building and house improvement on a grand scale and an obsession with perfection in everything from architecture to etiquette.

Visits to Hartsbourne were a nightmare for Blossom, with Maxine so withdrawn and silent. She was after all, eighteen at the beginning of 1920 and, after the war years, ready to be able to go out and have fun and spend time with her contemporaries.

She thought longingly of the days when she and other girls of her age had spent their summers at Frinton messing about on the

43

sands and gossiping. It was a tight little circle of friends, girls who were at school with her, other theatrical offspring, Diana Bancroft (grandaughter of the great "Squire Bancroft"), Jan Du Maurier, younger sister of Daphne and so on.

At Hartsbourne the weekend house parties were kept up but instead of the old Friday-to-Monday routine, the guests were not expected to arrive before Saturday lunchtime at the earliest and had to go on Sunday night. The rest of the week Blossom had to spend often alone with her aunt (apart from the many servants, of course), or sometimes with one or two of Maxine's close lady friends who felt sorry for her. Bridge became an end in itself for Maxine and this was obligatory for anyone who stayed. Blossom did hold out against this and positively refused to learn to play, so did all her sisters as well. So for Blossom the evenings were still more boring than the days.

Maxine took Blossom with her when she went to St. Moritz and Cannes, but even there she spent nearly all the time in her hotel room playing bridge and other card games. Occasionally the gloom lightened and, if her aunt thought that she was perfectly properly chaperoned, she was allowed to go out and Blossom really loved that.

The spell that Maxine apparently cast over all and sundry did affect Blossom; she longed to please her aunt, but somehow everything she tried she found her aunt disapproved of or was dismissive of, especially about her hair, her face, her clothes. There was just no answer to it.

When Maxine decided to sell Hartsbourne, a new problem awaited the Forbes-Robertson family.

The picture painted of Aunt Maxine thus far is not entirely sympathetic but we must be fair to her. Violet Bonham Carter said of society ladies at the time that few if any were "snowdrops," most were "thoroughly versed in the life of the jungle." She remembers the intense admiration that Winston Churchill had for Maxine. He said: "a great and valiant woman," a tigress carrying her little sister Gertrude "through the jungle of life" like a cub in the tigress's mouth, protecting her from "the ferocities and perils she had herself encountered" and had to deal with.

Oswald Mosley was another who fell under Maxine's spell, or she under his, or perhaps both. He was notoriously fickle and a womaniser of the 'n'th degree but Winston Churchill remained loyal to her.

The extent of Winston Churchill's friendship can be traced from at least 1911 until her death. In 1911 on the 25th June he was writing to his wife from Hartsbourne Manor where he was staying, thus:

"My darling Clemmie,

Maxine is so nice. She has a new bullfinch – it arrived only last night and already it sits on her shoulder and eats seeds out of her mouth.

Maxine sends you her best love. She and I spent a long time last night singing your praises. Did the Cat's ear burn!"

In 1915 Winston visited Maxine in Belgium even though the first World War was raging in that area. Spiers who was with him wrote in his diary of "Maxine Elliot, Churchill's friend of many years":

"Tea with Maxine Elliot on her barge, nice clever woman, must have been v. beautiful."

In 1914 she organised a Belgian Relief Barge, from which in 15 months she fed and clothed some 350,000 refugees. Blossom's concern for the refugees in the second World War and her personal assistance of many had its roots thus firmly established.

Churchill met his great friend Lord Thurso at Maxine's house "near Maidenhead."

By 1937 it was being said that "Clemmie does not like Maxine," therefore she was not at Maxine's Château in company with the Duke and Duchess of Windsor, Churchill and other such high-fliers. Vincent Sheean, who was variously an author, journalist and war correspondent, also spent a lot of time at the Château. He had married Blossom's youngest sister Diana (Dinah) in Vienna in 1935, so presumably Diana was there as well although she does not seem to be recorded in the memoirs of the notable.

James Vincent Sheean, who used Vincent as his professional name but was always called Jimmy by his family and friends, was an interesting, rather nebulous figure, an American of Irish extraction, and strangely enough his mother was a MacDermott; he was tall and good looking with, so it was said, " a map of Ireland on his face"!

Vincent Sheean would have had something in common with the Duchess of Windsor but the extent of their intimacy cannot be deduced from the records of them all in "Maxine's gold and white dining room." They paint only a picture of elegance and luxurious indulgence. Blossom, by then, was busy with more technical matters of business and commerce which were of greater satisfaction to her.

Maxine was what would nowadays be called "a control freak." Although the reasons for it were obvious and a cause for sympathy perhaps, the practice of it made all around her subject to her iron will and hardly anyone was able to stand out against her. Unless one has had an aunt like that, it is hard to understand how one person is able to wield such power. It was simply a way of showing her love for her family that she was unable to show in any other way.

She decided to leave Hartsbourne and have a London house. Hartsbourne was at Bushey Heath, Hertfordshire; even in those days it was less than an hour's drive from the centre of London. Nowadays it is not even as far out of London as Watford.

Maxine was rather jealous of the status of the 22 Bedford Square address and no doubt felt that she could or should "go one better" with regard to prestige. She wanted a place where she could reign over society without having actually to go anywhere herself. Of course it had to be a very large house to satisfy her ego, and the fact that she was going to be the sole occupant apart from the staff, who naturally did not figure in her calculations, was daunting even to her. Maybe she panicked at the thought of so much space surrounding her or maybe she always had the idea in mind that Johnston, Gertrude and the girls would live there with her if she offered inducements enough.

Anyway she said that it was obviously foolish for them to live in two very big houses, with all the expenses which she was so much more able to cover, and all the troubles of running such a house as 22 Bedford Square was only too apparent for poor Gertrude and so on and so on. The fact that Maxine was more efficient in these problems than Gertrude was true, and Gertrude was inclined to fall in with her sister's will, at the same time in a highly nervous state over what her husband would say.

Designing the house was a thing in itself for Maxine, with a suite for the Forbes-Robertsons (she had already had a suite built specially for them at Hartsbourne). Everything had been thought of, a nursery for the two youngest children, a study for "dear Forbie," and Blossom would have her very own drawing room where the dear girl could entertain her own young friends. At this point Blossom muttered: "Imagine me *daring* to do such a thing." This aside says more than a thousand descriptive words.

Maxine did not think that anyone would oppose her, so she calmly proceeded with her scheme. Blossom tried to tell her that she did not think her parents would agree but did not get a chance to finish the sentence. Maxine saw her chance as Gertrude and Jean had to be away on a long tour of Australia, and of course then the journey alone was weeks or even months long each way.

Johnston by then was in peaceful retirement and, for a while, unaware of just how much of the proposal had already been put in place; but when he did find out, he wrote a letter to Maxine of such controlled rage that the words themselves seem to be dancing off the page.

Addressing her as "My dear One" with a capital 'O,' he started off icily polite:

> "I fear you are under the impression that we are all to live together with you in your new house," *and that* "you, in your handsome fashion" *and so on. Significantly he says:* "I have spoken to Blossom on the subject and she is entirely in agreement with me."

When one considers that Blossom was then only just twenty-one and Johnston was nearly seventy, it looks as if Blossom was already having to take decisions and assuming an important role almost as the head of the family. No doubt this experience would stand her in good stead when she had the responsibilities of the future.

When Blossom became engaged to be married, Maxine again tried to take over her life, and designed and had constructed an apartment in her house for the bride and groom. Blossom was reduced to almost snivelling when saying: "But, but, we want a house of our own."

Luckily for Blossom just at this time, her sister Jean's acting career was beginning to burgeon and so Maxine turned her full attention onto Jean. Eventually when Jean came to be married to James Hamilton, Maxine was up to her old tricks and bought a beautiful house for them at Grove End Road in St. Johns Wood near Regents Park as a wedding present. Someone had to tell her that they would not accept and this task fell to Jamie Hamilton who, as he had not had much contact with Maxine up till then, hardly knew what he was up against.

There is very little information available on how and when Blossom met Inigo Freeman-Thomas, always known as "Nigs," but just slightly less than two years after the great contretemps between her Aunt Maxine and her father over where they should live she was married to him.

The marriage took place on October 8th 1924 after the requisite calling of the banns at the parish church of St. Mark at Hamilton Terrace, which is just off Maida Vale in London. Both the residences of the bride and the groom are given as Hamilton Terrace and one wonders why this should have been so, especially as by the time she was married for the second time her address was given as 22 Bedford Square. Was Maxine again manipulating the venues?

Inigo Brassey Freeman-Thomas, his age given as twenty-five, bachelor, was described in the 'rank or profession' as simply "Peer's son." His father was Freeman Viscount Willingdon, "Peer of the Realm." Blossom, given her full name, Maxine Frances Mary Forbes-Robertson, twenty-three years old, spinster, no profession given, and her father simply decribed by name and "Knight." It must have looked an ideal match.

It may be that the wedding was conducted by a bishop, or perhaps the vicar's surname may have conveniently been "Bishop" as the celebrant's name was Henry Whitehead Bishop. Aunt Maxine managed to get in on the act, as she was one of the witnesses on the marriage certificate along with Marie Adelaide Willingdon and J. Forbes-Robertson.

Meanwhile her sister Jean's talents were blooming. Maxine probably liked to think that she had a great hand in her success but her talents were those more closely related to her father's sensitive acting skills rather than her Aunt's flamboyant, compelling attractions. Adjectives used by the critics were of the following: "incandescent," "shimmering," "magical." She had enormous success in such plays of depth as *"Hedda Gabler," "Romeo and Juliet," "Twelfth Night," "Berkeley Square"* (this was called an "unearthly" performance), and then she was instrumental in commencing the triumph of J.M. Barrie's *"Peter Pan,"* a success which has continued to this day. Aunt Maxine continued to bug her with such comments as "your nose looks too big" or "that pink dress is ghastly," but at the same time she wrote to Louis Levy that "Jean is playing like an angel."

Jean was really the only one of the family who could stand up to Maxine and be psychologically unaffected by her. Although shy and private she had the inner strength and confidence to be objective.

All this was rather hard for Blossom to bear. Having only one eye, a theatrical career was unlikely for her and she really needed an outlet for her energies and intellect. It is always difficult for an older sister seeing a younger sibling making such an impact on the world. Blossom had many skills but there seemed no way to put them into use.

She had become Viscountess Ratendone, but it was apparently an empty life. One might have expected her to become involved in motherhood and raising little viscounts and honourables to carry on the line but she told a close friend that Nigs was "impotent."

This could have many meanings, physical, psychological or just a matter of inclination, we can never be sure, but certainly when after their divorce Inigo married again (actually to Daphne Caldwell, sister of the famous Diana who was to become Lady Delamere amongst other titles and was notoriously involved in the "Happy Valley" Kenya set and the murder of Lord Errol) they never did have any children. We cannot prove these implications one way or the other but it must appear that Blossom was not happy about the situation.

However when Nigs' father, Lord Willingdon, was to be made Viceroy of India, something which had always fascinated her gave her an outlet for her own talents.

CHAPTER 4

OPPOSITES ATTRACT

The scene now moves to Sussex. So much of Blossom's life revolved around London but Sussex, and particularly Shoreham in Sussex was to play a big part in her life, not once, but several times.

Inigo Freeman-Thomas was to become a director of Southern Aircraft Ltd based at Shoreham Airport, a delightful airfield, quite near the sea; it is now jointly owned by the local councils, but in those days it was a little independent field run by a small flying club. Whether or not Nigs' interest in the club and the firm was in fact fired by Blossom's enthusiasm, it looks likely. In 1941 he succeeded to the title of Marquess, the second Marquess of Willingdon, but that is a long way ahead of our tale and that title is now extinct.

*   *   *

References to Blossom's life during her first marriage allude to the facts that she had already made her mark *as an amateur* in the fields of costume designing, woodcut engraving and gardening. There is no real data on these aspects of her talents but she may have had some hand in designing costumes for the stage, as she had at least two relatives actively engaged in the theatre and several friends. Perhaps she illustrated a book; it would be interesting to come across material to confirm this. They all seem to be the sort of pastimes eminently suitable for a wife in her strata of society.

A contemporary said that Blossom had "lots of affaires." At this distance we could hardly guess whether she meant frivolous or serious affairs. The society ladies amused themselves with little flirtations; the aftermath of the first World War had left a generation desperate to have a good time and make up for what they had missed. So many young men lost their lives in the war that morals had been replaced by *laissez faire* and Aunt Maxine's example was hardly one of Victorian values.

There was a "terrible scandal," to quote the Sunday paper *"The People,"* concerning Edwina, Countess Mountbatten and the coloured actor and singer, Paul Robeson; and Nancy Cunard and even Blossom herself had their names linked with this charismatic, talented man. Although there was a famous court case at which Lady Louis Mountbatten won the judgement against *"The People"* there was more substance to those allegations than those against Nancy Cunard. Certainly Peggy Ashcroft had a love affair with Paul, and Flora Robson too, but there is no real evidence to link Blossom with him except hearsay and the fact that they did meet and have friends in common.

Strangely, the prestigious theatre critic James Agate compared Robeson with Johnston Forbes-Robertson, using Johnston as a yardstick by which to judge all acting. Later Blossom's brother-in-law, André Van Gyseghem, having by then become the second husband of sister Jean, also had a hand in Paul Robeson's career.

If there was indeed any substance in the rumours we could not blame Blossom for her interest in this magnetic giant.

It was said that on both sides of the Atlantic "Paul was adored by all the women he ever met. Women absolutely swooned over Paul. Paul was pursued and sometimes caught. You'd have to be a saint not to fool around." This was his wife Essie writing, his "long-suffering wife" one might suppose, but it was not quite like that. Paul always thought that he had been entrapped into marriage by Essie, and she seemed happy to bask in the reflected glory and fame he engendered. When they were in England she wrote: "He's fallen in love with another girl – honest – besides the one he was in love with when you were here."

There are a lot of letters written to Robeson by Blossom's sister Jean, but strangely these seem to indicate a polite, rather distant friendship. This was before she married André Van Gyseghem; nevertheless he was involved in the close theatrical circle and was enormously impressed with Paul Robeson's talents. Mrs Patrick Campbell, George Bernard Shaw, Flora Robson, Noël Coward, all the notable contemporaries of the theatre were in the tight-knit group which included Blossom and Paul. Aunt Maxine alone stood apart: as an American she could not pay court to "a black man."

*   *   *

However the event which was to change Blossom's life so dramatically, and the lives of many others too, started dramatically enough in itself.

Shoreham airfield had some dangerous ditches surrounding it – well, dangerous to the little aircraft of the early thirties anyway, and a de Havilland Cirrus Moth G-EBZG crashed into one of these ditches and was more or less a complete wreck, its flimsy and light-weight construction looking like matchwood.

The flying club at Shoreham had been formed on a shoestring by enthusiasts including Fred Miles. The club bought this wrecked aircraft for next to nothing and set about rebuilding it for club use. Soon after this two new members joined the flying club: they were Nigs and Blossom. Nigs decided to buy this little aeroplane because Blossom wanted to learn to fly.

By coincidence, Claude-Graham White had performed some of his flying activities in this area, including a race with a boat, a motor cruiser belonging to a local hotelier!

Winston Churchill had also visited Shoreham in 1914 and narrowly escaped being involved in a 'heavy landing' in a strange-looking aircraft, an Annular Monoplane.

Blossom's first flying lesson took place on June 2nd 1930. The aircraft was an Avro 504K G-EBYB. Her flying instructor was Fred Miles.

She went solo on July 25th after fifteen hours and seventeen minutes. I guess fifteen hours and seventeen minutes is quite long enough to fall in love but concentrating on learning to fly at the same time seems a difficult feat.

Fred Miles built his first aircraft in his father's laundry at Portslade. Now to Blossom's family the 'laundry' would merely be a room among many in the servant's quarters where the washing was done, but to Fred's family the 'Laundry' was their father's business and the means of maintaining him and his brothers.

Blossom had three sisters, Fred had three brothers. They were both the eldest of the family. Blossom was tall and slim, Fred was described as "big Fred Miles," "burly Fred Miles." He was not actually that large but he gave the impression of being so. His son, Jeremy, has said that his father's "burliness" was due to his having had to hump half-hundredweight laundry baskets up and down stairs in his youth.

Fred was born on February 22nd 1903, so was eighteen months younger than Blossom.

The laundry business was quite a good line to be in, long before the days of automatic washing machines. Starched shirts and linen sheets, all the paraphernalia of table napkins and such required regular laundry collections from even the most modest of middle-class households. Nevertheless the first World War had caused a recession in a great many businesses and money was quite short in the Miles family. Fred had to leave school early to earn money. He had an entrepreneurial streak in him from boyhood. He hired out a motorcycle to his friends at sixpence a head; from this he progressed to an ancient decrepit van, a Ford Model T, but this expired and was completely past any repairing. He gave up on such ventures and got a job as a projectionist in a local cinema near Brighton.

One thing is certain: Blossom had never met anyone like him.

In 1921 the breakthrough came for Fred. Two aviation-minded individuals, Fred Wallis and Charles Gates, had been building an aircraft, a biplane, but during the war it had been impossible to complete it and they had to decide what to do with the bits and pieces that comprised their efforts.

They got together in a shop at Portslade, and by some chance, Fred Miles happened to be there as well. Fred had been building a sports car or possibly rebuilding one and the result of the rendez-vous was that Fred Miles swapped his half-built sports car for a half-built aeroplane. He was only eighteen years old at the time.

It takes some time to build an aeroplane, especially with no money, so it is a wonder that the youthful Fred did not lose interest in the project, and he may have done so temporarily because it is not until 1925 that there seems to be any real progress on the aircraft. Even then it was not complete, and evidently he must have persuaded Fred Wallis to part with some components of the original sports car as the longerons for the aircraft were actually taken out of the sports car. He called it the "Gnat" and he got one of his brothers, Dennis, in on the scheme and also a friend, Reuben

Hart. The Hart family was to feature in future Miles developments as did the Gates family. Fred still had to learn to fly.

There are a few tales about Fred having a joyride in an aircraft at Brighton and that this is what sparked his interest in flying, but there is no hard data on that and in those days most youngsters jumped at the chance of such a jaunt, more or less on the level of a ride on a roller-coaster or having one's palm read at the fair; so it is extremely likely that he did pay his five shillings for this sort of experience. But it appears that he was always interested in things mechanical; he may have been involved in repairing his father's laundry equipment, and aircraft were the new, exciting craze, and any feats of daring or endurance concerning flying made headlines.

It is unlikely that there were any detailed drawings of the Gnat, so probably it was mainly in a practical capacity that Fred Miles was involved, and this suited him and his skills. He employed a second-hand propeller and an engine as small as would now power a motor-cycle or a microlight aircraft, but . . . it never flew.

Strange to say, this did not seem to dampen Fred Miles' enthusiasm; he was desperate to learn to fly, but how?

There had been a flying school at Shoreham before the first World War run by Cecil Pashley. Pashley was 'the grand old man' of the early flying days and is still honoured today for his achievements. Fred tracked him down in London in 1925 and somehow managed to persuade him to cooperate in a venture with him, although by then Cecil Pashley at thirty-four was old enough to be more cautious in his business affairs.

The twenty-two-year-old Fred Miles not only persuaded Pashley to set up a partnership with him but also persuaded his own father to provide the finance!

They entered upon a business to provide a flying school and a joyriding facility. They had one ancient aeroplane and no site or premises. The one aircraft was the Avro 504K G-EATU belonging to Pashley that had seen many flying hours already and was considerably out of date, having been designed along the lines of the prewar biplanes; it was eventually to come to grief, crashing on the Sussex downs in 1928.

The aeroplane was flown down from Hendon by Pashley and he had to land on a sloping field north of Southwick. The aircraft then had to be dismantled and taken down to the laundry, where it was overhauled and put together again. This took a long, long time and of course, even in those days, aircraft had to satisfy the inspectors from the Air Ministry on their airworthiness. Fred was very dependent on his father both financially and technically; he obviously was not earning any money and it must have disrupted the laundry business considerably to have an aircraft lurking amongst the washing, and tools and oily bits and pieces all over the place.

Fred Miles Senior is indubitably one of the unsung heroes of aviation.

Another proof of Fred Junior's persuasive powers is that he managed to get a notoriously difficult and anti-flying farmer to lease a field with a barn to the newly-formed company. They called the company the "Gnat Aero Company" and installed the Avro 504K in the barn and started business. Well, just how much business is not hard to imagine – not much, we guess.

On November 24th 1925 the aircraft was airborne, flown by Cecil Pashley with a "passenger." The most likely passenger by far would have Fred, but there is no proof of that. On November 26th 1925 Fred had his first flying lesson. Keen as he was after all the delays, by the end of 1925 Fred had only done 3 hours with Cecil. This seems strange but perhaps the weather was bad or it may simply have been that they did not have enough money for fuel or spares, or they may have been too busy trying to drum up business or sponsors. Certainly they had to install a barbed-wire fence to keep the farmer's cows off the field. This would have occupied a lot of their time and effort, and money as well.

Fred did not actually go solo until May 19th 1926, after 15 hrs 24 mins dual. Blossom's prowess seems even more impressive in the light of this, but circumstances were obviously to be very different.

They had only four pupils when they started the flying training school, not enough to keep body and soul together, let alone aeroplanes. The Air Ministry was not very helpful, as they were to prove at a much later date, and would not grant a licence to use the field as an aerodrome.

In spite of all these setbacks they plodded on and indeed bought some more aircraft. Claude Graham-White then sold his company at Hendon (the hangar is still to be seen a couple of hundred yards from the Royal Air Force Museum), so Fred and Cecil bought two more curiously out-of-date aircraft from him. One was a Bantam, and the other the really ancient Graham-White Boxkite.

A casual observer might have thought that they were about to set up a museum instead of a flying school, but no doubt they had to get what they could afford and what was available. However along with these purchases they did obtain a lot of spares which could be usefully emended. Next they bought an old canvas Bessoneaux hangar such as had been used in the field during the first World War.

A strange ill-assorted collection of buildings and aircraft thus grew up. Who would have taken them seriously?

Cecil Pashley's wages were only £3 per week and apparently Fred had no salary but took what expenses he needed; living at home, maybe he didn't need much. Pashley probably had to pay for parts and fuel and other aviation costs out of his £3.

Alliot Verdon Roe had a factory at Hamble near Southampton but had decided to concentrate his aviation activities in Manchester. So the Avro factory was turned over to the Air Service Training Company and this gave Fred and Cecil the opportunity to buy some more aeroplanes at knock-down prices.

With only one Avro 504K, they were lucky to be able to construct another one from spares bought from A.V. Roe – this was G-EAJU – and they also bought two other Avro types, a Baby, G-EAUM, and a Triplane, G-EAUJ. Some Baby components were also purchased (or "acquired," the records say!) and these were to be useful later when Fred was producing the Southern Martlet.

In April 1926, Fred still hadn't got his pilot's licence, but such was the faith and enthusiasm that they rented another field; this was larger than the previous farm one but it was still only a quarter of a mile long and less than half that wide. Moving all their bits and pieces and their canvas hangar must have taken time and ingenuity. Presumably the barn had to stay with the farmer, but they still had enough energy left to lobby the local brewer to 'cough up' some money (only a hundred pounds) towards a clubhouse, and they also decided to build two more hangars.

The beginning of May saw the general strike throughout the land, and although this was obviously a big problem in getting fuel and other necessities, and also transport to and from the field for both staff and clients, in a way it helped things for Fred and Cecil financially; in fact, it may have set them up in their business.

Strike-breaking occupied the resources and ingenuity of people like newspaper owners, so the *"Daily Mail"* was being printed in France and then copies of the paper were flown over to England by Imperial Airways. The new field at Shoreham was a convenient place to land, although the de Havilland aircraft used (a DH.34B) was a large ten-seater and must have been quite difficult to bring in for a safe landing and even more difficult to take off as the prevailing winds were often strong off the sea and would not have been directionally helpful.

When the papers had been off-loaded, Fred then drove them into Brighton for sale. Obviously, in the climate of the day, the proprietors of the *"Daily Mail"* would have been willing to pay quite a lot of money for this service. This proved to be a short-lived source of income, but the sight of the DH.34B and the sound of its Napier Lion engine with its 450 horse power roaring through the skies counted for the prestige and awareness of aviation at Shoreham.

After the general strike was over Fred seemed to have enough money to launch the new airfield as an 'aerodrome.' There were rumours that he had gone solo illegally early one morning before he had got his licence and I think this is in keeping with his character and youthful zest for adventure. Again the word "acquire" appears in their records, as they acquired two more aircraft, two Centaur IVs. These were biplanes built at Northolt (London) in 1919, so quite up to date as far as Fred was concerned. They were easy to fly and the handling was kind, the ideal aircraft in which to introduce passengers to the joys of flying.

Having gone solo officially in the Avro 504K G-EATU, in no time at all he was teaching others to fly; by May 24th he had only four minutes dual in the Centaur G-EALL with Pashley, but this was evidently enough for him to fly it on three very short flips on his own, and by June 5th he took a passenger up in it.

I think all these facts about Fred's early life show how very differently he would have approached a relationship with Blossom than Blossom herself would have seen a relationship with him, with her own sophisticated upbringing and the upper-class attitudes that must, of necessity, have coloured her psyche.

It is essential to continue exploring Fred's business life (one can hardly call it his career at this stage) in order to understand Blossom's development when she came under his influence and when he came under hers. The latter premise also contributed to her future.

The authorities – the chief authority concerned in these events being the Air Ministry – took a very dim view of what was going on at Shoreham: there were plenty of crashes, many fatal, among the light aircraft in the twenties and the Air Ministry did their best to keep entrepreneurs like Fred under scrutiny, if not under control. There had been, for some years then, a system of licences and certificates set up which should be rigidly complied with, but as far as we can find out the certificates of airworthiness for each of the aircraft seemed to be conspicuous only by their absence and no one seemed to possess an engineer's licence necessary to work on a 'plane. As far as pilot's licences went, to fly paying passengers or 'flying for hire or reward' required a 'B' licence: well, Cecil Pashley had one of those, but Fred seemed to have only an 'A' licence.

The Air Ministry threatened to prevent the grand launch day of the aerodrome and sent a Bristol Fighter aircraft to investigate. It landed but the field was not long enough and it crashed into the ditch at the far end. What happened thereafter we don't know, but Fred and Co continued putting up posters in all the likely local spots advertising the grand opening day and thought that the Air Ministry had forgotten about them.

They were horrified on the actual day of the launch when they saw another Bristol Fighter flying round and round looking ominously as if it was 'casing the joint,' but they were even more horrified when with only one hour to go before the grand opening, it came in and landed.

Forunately – very fortunately – it landed without mishap because it contained the dapper Director of Civil Aviation himself; this was Sir Sefton Brancker, who always affected a monocle.

Well, Fred and all the others thought that that was the end of all their hopes and careers, but Sir Sefton seemed to be highly amused and joked about Shoreham being "the Headquarters of the Independent Air Force" as they had no inspectors, inspections, engineers, licences or certificates. This genial man, who was probably just as instrumental in Fred and Blossom's lives as Fred's father had been and was to be, was killed in the crash of the R101 airship in 1930.

Sir Sefton could easily have closed them down then and there, but whether it was Fred's charisma or his intellect which impressed him, he gave useful advice and got a firm promise that affairs would be put in order and that things would be run on a businesslike and efficient system. He insisted that Fred should get his 'B' licence.

The flying diplay was evidently a great success. It is said that the RAF gave an aerobatic show but I wonder if this was just the lone Bristol Fighter. At any rate Fred took passengers up on six flights and it seems that this fired the enthusiasm of those who could afford it, because he did another five joyrides on the following day; these were all in the Centaur G-EALL.

The poor old Avro 504K was shortly to become another crash statistic when Cecil Pashley wrecked it in a ditch, having had the engine fail on take-off, a serious and often fatal event even in today's aircraft; but Cecil, at least, survived as indeed did his two passengers, employees of the Shoreham outfit. They were none of them unscathed but all were still alive. This was lucky on two counts, firstly that two key employees survived, and secondly that no notable or influential passengers were involved in the scare; the Avro was much later reincarnated from other bits and pieces.

Although the lucky part of the crash must have drawn sighs of relief from Fred, nevertheless it was a very heavy blow for their ongoing business. They just had to have another aircraft, so yet again Fred's dad was the saviour and came up with three hundred pounds, enough to buy another Avro. This one was purchased from Brooklands, where G-EBJE was available, having been owned by the racing driver John Cobb. (Incidentally one can still see G-EBJE in the museum at Hendon.)

Undeterred yet again, and probably on Sir Sefton's advice or instructions, Fred and Cecil divided the business up. They formed

The Southern Aircraft Company, which was the senior firm and took care of building aircraft (they already had their sights set high) and the engineering and maintenance of them, and a second company, more or less a subsidiary of Southern Aircraft, which was solely to run the flying club, giving lessons and joy rides: this latter firm was called the Southern Aero Club. Now although they both seemed to deem themselves "Limited" they were not actually registered as such until 1929. Rushing around bureaucracy and filling in forms was not a high priority with either Fred or Cecil, and the cost of registration may have been a deterrent.

So we have nearly come to the point which was to prove so significant, where Lord Inigo Freeman-Thomas came into the picture. The scene was set which led the way to him becoming a director of the Southern Aircraft Company.

In the interim they continued giving joyrides and flying lessons and cobbling components together when they could not afford to do proper repairs, and getting away with it, as Fred did one time when he had a replacement engine in the aircraft he was using to get the qualifications for his 'B' licence. The engine was so underpowered compared with the one which should have been installed (but which was unservicable) that he found he was practically going backwards, so he landed in a convenient field and slept the night under a haystack waiting for the winds to die down. And . . . nobody missed him.

A few things combined to help their enterprise in the next couple of years. Another joyriding firm called the Berkshire Aviation Co decided there was more business down on the Sussex coast than in deepest Berkshire where they had originally been founded, and so they obviously would have been a source of income when they carried on their flights from Shoreham, whether they paid rent or landing fees. Another significant happening was that Sir Alan Cobham, who at that time was one of the most famous names in aviation all round the country, was lobbying local and district councils to support flying in setting up municipal flying fields in the same way that they supported public parks.

A third thing that helped was the involvement of Lancing College. This is a prestigious college which anyone travelling near Shoreham cannot help noticing as it looks down from a high position on the downs above the airfield. The Lancing College contingent of the Officers' Training Corps took active parts in airshows and flying displays at Shoreham, which drew large crowds. The officer commanding this O.T.C., Major E.B. ("Gordo") Gordon, had been taught to fly by Cecil Pashley and was an old boy of Lancing College. Flight Lieutenant Luxmore was a skilled aerobatic pilot and gave exciting displays at the show. This introduced the precarious enterprise to the wealthier elements of society. Rich people started owning their own 'planes and keeping them at the field and flying them from Shoreham. Even coats of arms were now painted on owners' aircraft, inappropriate as they might have seemed – like *"Ferio et Feci."*

Don Brown had been involved with Miles' activities from the beginning, and was always an enthusiastic helper, although employed at the time in a gas works. Amongst other talents he possessed he was a mathematician, and so he taught Fred mathematics. This was now the end of the era when flying 'by the seat of one's pants' and surviving more by luck than judgement and 'guesstimating' in design was commonplace; all these things were to be outlawed, not only by the requirements of the Air Registration Board but also by sheer common sense as the numbers of aircraft and of people flying as passengers was about to increase by leaps and bounds.

Mathematics was now the king. Don taught Fred maths, and did Fred teach Blossom, or did Don Brown teach her himself? Before Blossom came on the scene Don Brown was quite amused at Fred's lack of knowledge of how to calculate, or even consider, the position of the centre of gravity, and even more amused to find that Fred's modifications and engine installations resulted in such errors in the crucial relation between centre of gravity and centre of pressure that they could hardly have been more wrong and yet . . . his aircraft seemed to fly perfectly!

But still we must go on with Fred's development, not just as a pilot and not just in the business field, but in that of his own character. Don Brown writes of those days as when "we had little knowledge, little money and lots of enthusiasm." The last two items were all too true, but I think he sells himself short when he refers to "little knowledge." Between them, these men at Shoreham in the late twenties had an immense amount of knowledge based on sheer experience and having to overcome handicaps which to the slightly less enthusiastic would have seemed insuperable. They had hard-won knowledge of a practical nature – which was invaluable – to add to theoretical knowledge yet to be acquired. This reverence for the practical basis of aviation, the groundwork, the hands-on experience was never to be lost by Fred. It manifested itself in his later career and in how he handled the apprentices and students of his Woodley days.

By 1928, with the experience gained in rebuilding and reconstructing the ancient types they had been of necessity saddled with, Fred felt able to set about designing and producing a new aircraft from scratch. The team involved included Don Brown, of course, and Fred's young brother George, who had been taken into the firm and was to prove an essential part of the later triumvirate. Harry Hull was the practical man and Ruben Hart, who had been a friend of the Miles family for years and had been involved earlier when brother Dennis Miles had also been associated, completed the quintet.

George Miles, a very different personality in both looks and character from Fred, is still alive today (1998) and continued working in aviation and aviation-related industry until well into his eighties.

The aircraft that they constructed was the Southern Martlet. Although it did not look all that different from previous biplanes, it was nevertheless an advance on the old types that Fred and Co had had to fly. It was very small, a single-seater, but proved to be highly manoeuvrable. The excitement of their very first production aircraft was not at all diminished by the fact the design was based on the Avro Baby or that it was a year in gestation.

The Martlet was financed by a 'rich young man,' Lionel E.R. Bellairs, who wanted an aeroplane of his own. A draughtsman had to be poached from Avro and his name was by coincidence Miles, Horace Miles, who was no relation as far as we know. The details of this Martlet are well documented in Don Brown's book *"Miles Aircraft Since 1925."* They made six of them. The first one (G-AAII) was registered in October 1929 and sold to Miss N.B. Birkett. The second, G-AAVD, was the one which Lionel Bellairs had (I wonder why he didn't have the first one? Possibly because Nancy Birkett was an employee), which had its Certificate of Airworthiness by March 24th 1930; the third, G-AAYZ, was owned by the Right Honourable F.E. Guest; the fourth, G-AAYX, by Flight-Lieutenant R.L.R. Atcherley; the fifth, G-ABBN, by the Marquis of Douglas and Clydesdale (later the Duke of Hamilton); and – then we come to the interesting bit – the sixth G-ABIF to Maxine Freeman-Thomas, the C. of A. being dated May 30th 1931. She was to give this aircraft to the Air Training Corps in 1940.

CHAPTER 5

FLYING VENTURES

Somewhere along the line there was an explosion waiting to happen. Two personalities were being moulded by circumstances as well as by their inheritance and ancestors.

Blossom had achieved her aunt Maxine's ambition in marrying a Lord, but had she achieved her own ambition? She had an uneasy feeling that she was not making the most of her potential in the pursuits of her social circle and the avenues open to her. Her father's status and undeniable greatness in his profession; her aunt's beauty and force of character; her mother's acting ability and at the same time her dithering over domestic and family details; her sister Jean's burgeoning talents and career; had she got to be satisfied with this?

Her interest in flying grew out of several of these factors. Sheer opportunism was one of these, but in the back of her mind, here was something that the rest of her family couldn't do. Owning an aeroplane, learning to fly it, this was something about which none of the others who influenced her had ever thought.

It was considered eminently suitable for a Viscountess to show an interest in aviation – it was, after all, a sport mainly open to the extremely rich. The Countess Drogheda had not only famously flown aircraft but had written an introduction to technical books on the subject and also written about *"War Balloons 1794 to 1865"* and *"The Earliest Parachute Descents 1783 to 1837,"* two very well-researched and erudite publications. Kathleen Drogheda was an intimate friend of her aunt's and she may have influenced Blossom and sparked her interest in flying more than anyone else.

Aunt Maxine implied that Blossom was extremely lucky to have secured a "Lord" in view of the fact that she didn't have any dress sense, did not achieve what Maxine considered "elegance," didn't "make the most of herself" and . . . only had one eye. Although in later years, as we have said, she did not seem to consider this a handicap, nevertheless young girls are very quick to feel their own imperfections, whether real or imaginary, and this certainly was an 'imperfection.' Apparently only Blossom's youngest sister Diana, known as Dinah, thought that Blossom was "beautiful" in the conventional sense of the word; the rest of her family seemed to tiptoe round the subject, not wishing to make her self-conscious about her eye, but by this 'walking on eggs' technique only giving weight to her own uneasy suspicions.

We can only guess what part, large or small, was played by Aunt Maxine in the matchmaking which resulted in Blossom marrying Inigo, and Blossom appeared to try to make a success of the marriage, but there were many clues to the fact that she was not happy. His nickname Nigs makes it all sound too much like a P.G. Wodehouse farce, but it is hard to judge the twenties' upper class social set-up from the distant view of the end of the century. We know that the young Blossom was a quiet, introverted girl and the glorious freedom represented by flying through the air held an enormous appeal for all the reasons outlined above.

Now Fred's character had been forged rather than moulded. As shown he would go to any lengths to achieve his aims. If it involved cutting corners, ignoring regulations, conning money out of his father, foregoing any personal comforts, food, shelter, whatever, well, so be it.

Guesswork comes into the calculations here, but certainly it does not look as if he would have had any time, money, opportunity or inclination for any girl friends or sex. I should be very surprised to learn otherwise. He had been plugging away at his chosen career and ambitions since he was in his teens and now, when he was on the brink of achieving some considerable status in the aviation world, it was all to be threatened by a love affair.

By the time that Fred and Blossom met, they had both overcome much adversity; at the same time both knew that there was much more to be achieved, but until they met they did *not* know that there was a great deal more adversity to overcome.

The build-up of both their characters was reaching a peak and when they were thrown together by a Fate which, although it seemed cruel at the time, was really totally benign, they both knew that this was 'the real thing.'

Too many words have been written about falling in love. It is ever to be regarded as nothing more than a literary cliché. We will not attempt to analyse it here, readers will be glad to know. Nevertheless what happened between them was an explosion of emotion, the time was ripe for it for both of them, and so . . . it happened.

Fred took it very badly: he felt guilt, fear, nervous of the reactions of all around him.

Now divorce was not unknown in the Forbes-Robertson and Elliot families, far from it. Blossom could probably cope with that side of the relationship. Fred, however, although we know little about his mother and only that his father was a 'soft touch' as far as money was concerned, lived in the stratum of society then known as small-time tradespeople, where divorce was a subject considered rather more disgraceful than blasphemy and a terrible stain on the character.

What was to affect Fred more than his family's disapprobation was the business aspect. Nigs was a director of the Southern Aircraft Company, perhaps the only director with any money. All he had worked for, all his hopes were now thrown in jeopardy by his love affair with Nigs' wife. Blossom however was in seventh heaven. She was to be loved for herself alone, she was not now to bathe only in the reflected glory of being the wife of a Lord. She had learned to fly an aeroplane, and she was good at it. The person who had taught her to fly must be imbued with a mystical significance which would outweigh all other considerations. Anything, anything at all was now possible.

Fred had a lot to lose; his business reputation had increased to such a point that the bank was willing to lend him £7,000 and in fact, did so. This sum represented an enormous investment in 1930 when one considers that £100 a year was a reasonable salary. They bought the one hundred and fifty acres of land necessary for their airfield and to establish an airport there. They managed to pay the interest on this sum until, with luck, and with their anticipated judgement, the combined councils of Brighton, Hove and Worthing decided it was the most suitable, and indeed, the *only* site for their Municipal Aerodrome. I think a lot of strings had to be pulled along the line, but no matter, their main aim had been achieved and for once they were set up according to all the necessary regulations.

Cecil Pashley still regarded Fred's escapades in the air as foolish and the activities of an irresponsible dare-devil, but Don Brown was ready for 'fun' and aided and abetted him. They had great scrapes and escapes with the aircraft which was the pivotal instrument in the involvement of Inigo and his wife in the flying club, the Cirrus Moth G-EBZG which the club had bought for £50 after it had crashed into the ditch and which was subsequently bought by Inigo Freeman-Thomas. This aeroplane was known as "Jemimah"; Fred thought "it might be fun to fly it in the dark" and so this was a first in night-flying experience for most of them. One night it was Don's turn; Fred told him to do his safety belt up tightly in case they finished up in the ditch, and indeed they nearly came to grief as Fred overshot the little field. But he managed to climb over the irritating ditch and do another circuit, and this time made a perfect landing assisted by three petrol flares. This was just as well, because the Moth was quite an advanced aircraft compared with most of their stock.

Don Brown always said that learning to fly at Shoreham was the best training in the world, because as the airfield was surrounded by ditches, if you didn't quickly learn to fly extremely well, you finished up in one of them. Thus, even a ditch was to play a part in our drama.

If Cecil Pashley disapproved of Fred's cavalier attitude to flying, he was only too ready to disapprove of his romantic involvement with the wife of a director of their company. He was not the only one to regard this in a censorious light. Fred could not cope with this pressure from all sides; it was something totally outside his experience and he felt that he had to find a solution. His solution and determination to 'do the right thing' led him to decide to resign from the Shoreham set-up and go abroad. In a short time, in a hurry that looked like panic, he sold up everything he had. The total proceeds of his life only amounted to enough to buy a Spartan aircraft. This was a two-seat biplane, similar to the Moth, and quite modern for Fred, as Simmonds Aircraft Ltd who afterwards called themselves Spartan was only formed in 1928; so it could not have been produced earlier than that and could even have been one of the ones built in 1931 after they moved from Southampton to the Isle of Wight. At any rate it was a good choice because although the design looked conventional enough it had all sorts of economy features like the rudder being interchangable with the tailplane! About fifty were constructed and they were quite successful even in the Arctic.

Fred had enough money to have this aircraft freighted to South Africa, then a colony and representing sunshine and super-opportunities for business; and he had enough money too for his own fare, so off he went to Cape Town. If he intended to send for Blossom once he got established, or whether his intention was to try to forget her or punish himself or whatever, we can only imagine.

This all happened in the summer of 1931; it was a hasty decision because as Don Brown says: "In a few weeks he was gone."

It was a great blow to those left at Shoreham. Fred had been the leader without a doubt. Nothing had quite the same urgency and impetus without him. They carried on, joyrides, training, all routine activities. Brother George was still in the set-up and he and the club secretary, quite formally addressed as Miss Birkett, took over the management of the flying club. The Southern Aircraft Company did not then seem to have such a high profile as the club, but it was still the parent body.

The employees and directors would probably have been very surprised to learn that their erstwhile positive and inspirational leader now found himself in a complete state of misery and indecision in South Africa. Lonely and distraught at being away from Blossom, he didn't give himself time to explore any of the projects or possibilities he had envisaged in the colony; but shortly after he landed in Cape Town, he sold the Spartan to pay for his passage on the first boat back home. Of course there may have been another factor in the equation, he may have had some news from back home as soon as he disembarked.

Meanwhile Blossom was going through the necessary procedures to obtain a divorce. Fred and Blossom were married on August 6th 1932 at the Registry Office in Holborn, London. Fred's age was given as twenty-nine, his condition "bachelor," his profession "Air Pilot," his residence as "11 Fitzroy Square, St. Pancras,

London," his father "Frederick Gaston Miles," and his father's profession as "Company Director."

The entries for Blossom can hardly be contained in the spaces provided on the certificate: "Maxine Frances Mary Freeman-Thomas formerly Forbes-Robertson (spinster)." Condition: "The divorced wife of Inigo Brassey Freeman-Thomas, Viscount Ratendone." Rank: "Viscountess." Residence: "22 Bedford Square, Bloomsbury." Father: "Johnston Forbes-Robertson." Father's rank: "Knight." Strangely she signs herself "Maxine Ratendone." The witnesses were her mother and her brother-in-law, James Hamilton. Blossom's age was given as thirty. It wasn't long before her thirty-first birthday.

One hurdle overcome, the next was to earn some money. This was a hurdle of some enormity. Not only did Fred now have a wife whom he obviously could not maintain in 'the manner to which she had been accustomed' but whom he couldn't maintain at all. His abortive foray to South Africa had used up any capital he might have had. Those who knew him at that time say that in spite of everything he still had confidence in his own ability, and we can see from the previous chapters that he had a gritty determination of quite heroic proportions. Whether Blossom had any money of her own is unclear. Her aunt had settled 'endowments' on the girls, but presumably they didn't come into these until she died, which didn't happen for another ten years. I can't imagine Blossom asking her Aunt for money, but of course she did have a great deal.

We will have to start calling Fred "Miles" now, because that is how he was known in the 'interregnum' before he became F.G. for the rest of his life.

Miles and Blossom brought diametrically opposed qualities together in their marriage and there can be no doubt that these qualities were responsible for the later success, but at first they contributed to the acceptance of any sort of adverse conditions like living in a caravan, which is what they did.

Living in a caravan in the spring and summer in Sussex with someone you love is the most romantic idyll imaginable, but in the winter? With very little money? With worries about the future? With all the slopping in and slopping out that goes with it? With muddy paths and waterlogged lanes? Earning a living was paramount to Miles. Paying his father back became quite an obsession. His father had had so much faith in Miles' schemes and plans that he didn't begrudge him either the money he had given and lent him or the other benefits that he had had in kind. Nevertheless Miles had always meant to pay him back with interest – he also had that much faith in his ventures. His father had never been wealthy in the sense of Blossom's relations and friends, he was getting older, Miles had a deep affection for him and was desperate to prove that he was worthy of so much trust. This was one of several factors that prompted him to set up all over again in the aviation business.

*   *   *

Miles and Blossom had an interim adventure which, although it did not make much money, provided them with vast amounts of aviation experience. They went 'barnstorming' in the spirit of Sir Alan Cobham's Flying Circus, which is still remembered today as an exciting exercise in popularising aviation. Giving joyrides to all and sundry in the most unlikely locations, zooming at low levels over countryside where the sparse inhabitants had never even seen an aircraft before, it was a crazy stunt. Often there was no set fee, just whatever anyone could afford. Sometimes three 'planes were involved, sometimes two and often by the end of the season there would be only one aircraft airworthy.

Miles and Blossom, Stephen Cliff and his wife Joan, Pauline Gower and Dorothy Spicer – they would set off into the unknown, land wherever they could and get bed and breakfast locally and fly off again the next day. Miles would fly one aircraft, Stephen Cliff another and Blossom and Joan Cliff would follow as best they could in Joan Cliff's MG, pick them up and look for a bed for the night.

Stephen Cliff was a young man of considerable means, in fact he later sold an *island* to Sir Alan Cobham, but he and his young wife had tremendous fun flying around the countryside with Miles and Blossom; they weren't quite sure if the two of them were married at that time or not, but the whole thing was such an adventure that such details were secondary, and whilst Blossom and Joan were careering round country lanes trying to find the fields in which their partners' 'planes had landed (or crashed) there was time for a lot of confidences to be imparted one to the other.

Pauline Gower was the pilot of the third 'plane of the circus with Dorothy Spicer her mechanic; Pauline Gower was to become very famous during the war when she was a vital member of the Air Transport Auxiliary and ferried 'planes to and from the dispersal fields. The two girls had decided that Pauline would qualify as a pilot while Dorothy would take qualifications as a ground engineer so that they could set up a business together. Pauline was the daughter of Sir Robert Gower, a Conservative member of Parliament. Pauline was only twenty-one in 1931; it had cost her £1 an hour to learn to fly and she had bought a Spartan two-seater to give joyrides. The barnstorming aerial circus of which they were part in 1931 is described as having "only three pilots" and a parachutist. I know nothing of the parachutist except that he or she must have been exceptionally brave, but the other two pilots referred to must have been Stephen Cliff and Miles, so it looks as if Joan Cliff's suspicions of whether Blossom and Miles were really married carried weight.

Pauline Gower and Dorothy Spicer were both full of fun and enthusiasm and they both had interesting careers, but it is a good job that they could not see into the future in those carefree, harum-scarum days because both died tragically and young.

Pauline had gone all through the war, flying all sorts of aircraft of all shapes and sizes with nothing to guide her except the briefest of pilot's notes. She was in the Air Transport Auxiliary from its inception on the first of December 1939 until the end of the war, when it was disbanded at the end of November 1945. In fact she was the Senior Commander. The choice of Pauline for this crucial role was influenced by the massive total of flying hours, more than 2,000, that she had built up in such jaunts and stunts as with Miles, Blossom and the Cliffs. She was awarded the M.B.E. in 1943. She fell in love and married Wing-Commander Bill Fahie in 1944 and died in childbirth after the war giving birth to twin boys.

Dorothy Spicer got her 'A,' 'B,' 'C' and 'D' ground engineer's licences and the two girls used up more of their nine lives with Campbell Black's Air Display, with many a bump and trip to hospital. She worked at Farnborough during the war but she too died soon afterwards in an air crash in South America, in which her husband Dick Pierce also died.

One of the barnstorming trips that the Miles and the Cliffs were involved in took then to Wales (Pauline and Dorothy did not go on this one, fortunately for them as it happened). They eventually found somewhere flat enough to land their little aeroplanes near the coast in mid-Wales. When the girls had caught them up in the MG, it was their responsibility to find somewhere to stay the night. This seemed impossible, the landscape and its inhabitants seemed so remote and even hostile. Eventually they did find something, but warned the menfolk that it "wasn't very nice." The men thought they were exaggerating, but when they got there they had to admit that it certainly *wasn't* very nice. It was actually filthy, but it was the only place, so that was that.

A further shock awaited them when they went to use the lavatory. It consisted of a wooden plank over a filthy bucket on an earth floor and, worst of all, there were three holes in this plank – a large hole, a middle-sized hole and a little hole.

"Just like Goldilocks and the three bears!" commented Joan Cliff.

They managed to think that this was a huge joke, but weren't quite sure whether it would be a suitable story to tell when they got home, if they ever did, as they were beginning to doubt by then. But . . . worse was to come.

As washing facilities were not just practically non-existent, they *were* non-existent, Joan thought it might be a good idea to go and have a swim in the sea which was not far away. Yes, it *was* a good idea until they got there and found how cold Cardigan Bay was.

"It's freezing!" said Miles; Blossom and Stephen refused to enter into the waves but Joan braved it and was glad later that she had.

During that period Blossom and Miles were staying with the Cliffs in their flat in Bristol. They had no other home then and were in semi-hiding. When they got back to Bristol Stephen was horrified, more than horrified, to find that he had caught crab lice, a particularly disgusting infestation, the only treatment for which at that time was to have one's most sensitive parts painted a violent purple. It wasn't long before both Blossom and Miles found that they had them too. They all put this down to using this dreadful wooden lavatory seat. It was probably more likely to have been sleeping in filthy bedsheets but who knows? Joan alone escaped this and she attributed her good fortune to having bathed in the sea as she was sure that the icy waters would have killed any parasites stone-dead.

And so the ups and downs of life 'on the road' continued. Blossom must have been reminded of her father's peripatetic life in the theatre, but Miles decided that some serious money-making enterprise was called for and therefore they rented a room above a shop in Sevenoaks in Kent. Somehow it was turned into a drawing office and the two of them began to design an aircraft.

The design they chose was to be called the "Satyr." Too much can be read into names, and the word "satyr" can have several meanings, two of which are almost completely opposite. As we all know it can mean a lecherous old devil, half man and half goat, and as such can mean "extremely wanton," but a satyr is also a butterfly and I would guess that it is the latter attribution that influenced Blossom. In fact it covers a family of butterflies, which in this country include the ringlets, the browns and the marbled white. Perhaps the gatekeeper butterfly inspired the name, or maybe it was more technical in the actual choice as the characteristic of the satyridae is that the veins of the forewing are swollen where they meet the thorax. They were to use the name of another butterfly species much later in the "Libellula."

Of course they had no facilities at all for building the aircraft once it had been designed, and it says much for their determination and powers of persuasion that Parnalls agreed to construct it for them. Miles had done some test-flying for them in the past but they were not actually building aircraft at that time. Maybe they needed the work anyway, because in no time at all the aircraft was not only designed, it was constructed and flying. Miles made the first flight in it in the early summer of 1932; it was registered G-ABVG.

George Parnall was in any case on much the same wavelength as Blossom and Miles; his had orginally been a wood-working firm which had been taken over, after which he then started up again and had made a few aircraft under contract in the first World War, but he was known mainly for his one-off efforts which had rather hilarious names such as the "Prawn," the "Possum," the "Plover" and the "Pixie."

Once again he was to be involved in a 'one-off' because only one Satyr was made. Nevertheless this was a successful aircraft. A nice, tidy little single-seater, it was very economical, very manoeuvrable and easy to fly and, although a biplane, looked very pretty. All the control wires were housed inside the wood and fabric fuselage, making it look more efficient and smacking of the attention to detail that came from Blossom's involvement in the design. Obviously they got the mathematics right because it was described as "delightful" to fly and was bought by Mrs Victor Bruce who operated her own flying circus. John Pugh used it for aerobatic displays which were really impressive and had the crowds applauding madly.

So many aircraft crashed in those days but the crash that saw the end of the Satyr was in no way the fault of the design either of the machine or of its construction.

One day in September 1936 Mrs Victor Bruce, who was flying the 'plane in a display, did not notice some telephone wires when she was coming to land until the last minute. The Satyr caught the wires, hung there for about thirty seconds, and fell to the ground. That was the end of the Satyr; Mrs Victor Bruce had slight concussion but lived to tell the tale.

However, before the demise of the Satyr, the 'plane had a very important part to play in Blossom's story. One late autumn day in 1932, Miles decided to fly the Satyr from Yate in Gloucestershire to Shoreham to show the aircraft to his parents. The Parnall factory was at Yate and no doubt the Satyr had been there for some servicing or similar reason.

I do not know what the range of the Satyr was, but with its little 75 horsepower Pobjoy engine and a cruising speed of 110 mph, it was probable that he would need a stop halfway. He decided to land at Woodley, about five miles from Reading to the south-east, more or less on his flight-line anyway. This is where fate took another hand in his life and in Blossom's life and in that of their children yet to be born. Bearing in mind that they had only been married in the August of that year, so much had happened already that it was almost impossible to grasp the acceleration to their fortunes that had already taken place and was about to erupt.

Woodley had always been a good place to land an aeroplane; as far back as 1913 Henri Salmet had landed his Blériot there and given joyrides. It was then known as Woodley Farm and was a flattish open area with not many trees and with a straight railway line nearby and the river Loddon (a tributary of the Thames), to act as convenient direction-finders.

Gustav Hamel had landed there in his brief aviation career and people like Cody flew in the Reading area, Alan Cobham in Northumberland Avenue, the Cornwall Aviation company by the river at Caversham; all sorts of oddities like manned kites in Palmer park sparked the imagination of the local people. The area which became Woodley aerodrome had been bought by a firm from Reading called Phillips & Powis (originally Phillips & Bloomfield) who had graduated from other forms of transport such as bicycles into aircraft when they got caught up with the current enthusiasm for anything to do with flying.

The appearance of Miles in his beautiful little Satyr would naturally have caused interest, and in the ensuing conversation Miles learnt that although Phillips & Powis had set up an embryo flying club and a flying training school, and had had air displays and open days to which the public had thronged in their thousands, they did not actually manufacture any aircraft there but merely repaired and serviced them. *They* did not have the background in aircraft design and construction, *Miles* did not have the premises or facilities necessary to put his ideas and designs into being, so therefore . . . it could be a perfect marriage. Two perfect marriages were thus implemented within a few weeks of each other.

Phillips & Powis were in a reasonably strong financial position, if on a small scale; Miles already had plans in his mind, if not on paper, for an aircraft which would be an improvement on the ubiquitous de Havilland Moth types. Miles put a good case before Phillips & Powis; soon the deal was done and Miles and Blossom moved to Woodley, which was then known as Reading Aerodrome.

This was just what Miles had been looking for, and we wonder if it was simply a coincidence that he had landed there, or had he done any homework beforehand? Did Blossom have any connections in the area which would have prompted such a project? Anyone associated with aviation would have heard about Woodley,

I am sure, because only the previous year Douglas Bader had crashed his Bristol Bulldog there, losing both his legs. At any rate, once the approach was made, a business-like agreement was set up and Miles and Blossom were on their way.

In the negotiations between Miles and Charles Powis, into which Blossom also entered, Powis was impressed with Miles' ideas for this aircraft which he saw as an alternative and superior vehicle to the Moth series. De Havilland by that time had a lot of backing behind them and Geoffrey de Havilland was credited, and rightly so, in being the foremost designer and manufacturer in the light aircraft field. However they were sticking with the biplane design, mainly because many people in both civil and military aviation thought that biplanes were of a sounder construction and therefore safer and more efficient than monoplanes.

It is easy for us at the turn of the twenty-first century to see that they were wrong, but in the early thirties monoplanes seemed futuristic and looked like science fiction to a lot of folk. Miles and Blossom convinced Powis that the monoplane was aerodynamically sound and that the design would necessarily be much cheaper to build; however the theories of structures and the stressing of them were in their infancy as far as practical aviation was concerned, so they did not put too much emphasis on the increased strength which would be needed for the components of the wings and the attachments thereof and the need for specialised materials, some of which were then not yet available.

The idea of actually becoming an aircraft manufacturer appealed to Powis, so he magnanimously agreed to let Miles have a corner of his hangar. Blossom and Miles started work straight away on the design of an aircraft that they were to call the "Hawk" and which was to be the basic design of many future light aircraft as they developed their ideas and improved the airframes.

The whole thrust of their argument was that they could produce an aircraft which would not only have a higher performance but which would be *cheaper*. The price of the Satyr had been £600 and, as we saw, only one was sold. It is hard to believe that they made a profit on this, or that it would have provided them with a living, even for a short time. The idea of being able to produce an aircraft considerably cheaper than the Satyr was partly dependent on establishing a market for a large number. Production lines were far into the future but the cost of the components and in particular the engines meant that breaking even was going to be difficult, let alone making a profit.

Yet another fortuitous circumstance came to bear on the project. The financial demise of a Canadian company meant a boost for Blossom and Miles. The Canadian firm had ordered a lot of engines, fifty in fact, of the Cirrus IIIA. This was an efficient little four-cylinder engine which developed 95 hp, absolutely ideal for their purposes and, having been introduced in the Mk. III form in 1928, it was well-tried and tested by already having been installed in such aircraft as the Avro Avian and the Westland Widgeon; some Moths also had the Cirrus II. The Cirrus was made by the Cirrus-Hermes Engine Co: it was really the engine which made private flying a possibility. Its rival when it was first developed in 1925, the Gnome rotary engine, developed hardly more than half the power of the Cirrus, and the practical and engineering problems of having the whole engine whizzing round and round can be imagined even by the uninitiated.

The Cirrus-Hermes Engine Co. was housed at Croydon and was formed in 1920 by a syndicate which included Colonel Darby and the (then) Mr Frederick Handley Page, who was to loom large (and he *was* very tall, too) in Blossom's and Miles' later years. It was on to a winner with the Cirrus, and so was Miles when he put in a bid for the liquidated stock of them because he got them extremely cheaply.

Thus Blossom and Miles had the perfect engine at the perfect price, and they had fifty of them; things could not have been going better, and they were getting on with their design. The mathematics taught them by Don Brown were standing them in good stead and they were working night and day with great enthusiasm but with very careful regard for safety. Having worked out the necessary strength for a particular component, they applied a reserve factor much higher than would be practical nowadays. One might think that this would result in a clumsy, stoutly-braced craft but they had such innovative ideas and their use of materials was imaginative to say the least. Even the engine mountings were made of wood!

The result was an aircraft of such classic simplicity and clean lines that it shouted of aerodynamic efficiency. They had intended to call it the "Ibex"; the thinking behind that is obscure, at least to me. Maybe it was because it reminded them of a holiday in the Alps, but then they thought that the name might be confused with a now long-forgotten aeroplane, the Hinkler Ibis. What's in a name? We keep inferring that, but the Hawk, as it was named, was to become their theme and their trade mark.

Phillips & Powis was still the company behind them and the firm retained the name for several years to come, but the aircraft were also prefixed with the Miles name. In October 1932 Harry Hull was persuaded to join Phillips & Powis from the Southern Aircraft Company; details on this are not clearly available but there did not seem to be any great problem. At the time George was still running Southern Aircraft Ltd and the Southern Aero Club and Don Brown must still have been there also. George did not actually wind up business at Shoreham until 1936, when he ensured that there was continuing employment for Cecil Pashley with the Brooklands School of Flying, which had taken over the old club. He then joined Blossom and Fred Miles at Woodley as Manager and Test Pilot in charge of engine development. However there seems to have been a lot of liaison between both George and Don and Fred Miles throughout this period because they were both at Woodley at various times. Although Harry Hull was now quite elderly, his woodworking and carpentry skills were such that he only needed a fourteen-year-old boy to assist him and construction proceeded at a pace sufficient to keep up with the design.

The principles of spruce frames covered by plywood to give maximum strength with minimum weight can be explored in many technical manuals for those who are interested, but for the others they can take it as read because the first prototype Hawk flew successfully without any modifications.

This first flight occurred on March 29th 1933, typically "at sunset." After only one minute of what was supposed to be a taxying test Miles was airborne! Impatience? Foolhardiness? Impetuosity? Or simply sheer confidence in himself, his aircraft and his wife? Typical also of their impatience, its own undercarriage was not yet completed so it took off and landed on an undercarriage 'borrowed' from a Spartan. And again, talking of impatience, within one week the Hawk had been flown by no less than fifty-three different pilots. Where on earth did they all come from? Don Brown was one of them and brother George another. What utter confidence was shown by both Blossom and Miles and those fifty-three pilots in that brand-new 'plane. Industrial espionage and inter-company rivalry did not seem to be too important at that time amongst aircraft manufacturers, because included in those brave fifty-three were all the test pilots from de Havillands and even Geoffrey de Havilland Senior and Geoffrey de Havilland Junior.

The performance was so much better than any comparable available biplane that there was a bit of a panic about the control surfaces; the Hawk was being compared to racing aircraft like the Comper Streak, and the concern was that it too would experience the flutter at high speeds which made this aircraft so vulnerable and dangerous.

Once again Miles answered those criticising and calling for mass balancing of the control surfaces by climbing the Hawk to 10,000 feet, putting its nose down and diving it to its terminal velocity! And . . . this was the first time he had ever worn a parachute in his life. Did that imply that his confidence was not quite so great as he intimated or did Blossom insist on it? Anyway no flutter and no other problems except, I should think, for the beating of his heart, and there was probably more flutter amongst those watching on the ground than on the ailerons and elevators of that tiny wooden 'plane. It was just as well because I doubt if a parachute would have done him any good in those circumstances, even if he had had time to have any parachute training.

They were able to sell this aircraft for £395, only later raising the price to £450 when the market was established and the supply of the cheap Cirrus engines was exhausted. So the orders poured in. Forty-seven Hawks were sold in Great Britain alone in fifteen months, fifteen months of frenetic activity for the team and even more so for Blossom. She had to find a house and sort out all the domestic details that go with the necessary social and business activity, and often those two were interchangeable.

A photograph of the prototype Hawk in 1933 shows Miles, Charles Powis and Harry Hull standing by the 'plane, while

Blossom, resplendent in helmet and goggles, is in the cockpit smiling broadly.

Flying was popular but not fully understood by many, as shown by the fact that one purchaser complained that flying in the Hawk had made his teenage daughter's underwear dirty. It was unfortunate that this irate father chose the exact time when Blossom and Miles were in deep discussion with an Air Ministry official who was to give the 'ay or nay' as to whether they would get the accreditation known then as 'design approval.' It was even more unfortunate for the poor girl as her father lifted her dress and showed her oil-stained knickers.

Another purchaser did not come up with the money for his Hawk, and Miles and friends stole it back one dark night out of a padlocked shed protected by barbed wire, which meant that Miles had to fly it around and around in the dark until it was light enough to land it back at Woodley. Once again his luck held and there was enough fuel in the tank to do this.

Think of the numbers of solicitors and legal bills concerned in a similar repossession today!

CHAPTER 6

THE MOVE TO WOODLEY

By 1934 Blossom and Miles had had a magnificent house built less than a mile from the airfield at Woodley. It was called "Lands End House," not because of any deep symbolic significance but merely because it was near an area called Lands End, and that in itself was because the lane at that point ended in a ford across the River Loddon. The public house at the ford is also called "The Lands End" but which was the chicken and which was the egg? Geographically it is in Twyford but in actuality it is much nearer to Woodley.

The house is still there today and became a listed building in 1986; and although one might think that it is typically 'thirties' architecture, it has a unique quality very different from the 'Odeon' school of the time. The architect was Guy Morgan; he was very young and Lands End House was his first major contract. Many of the other buildings on the factory site were also designed by him and his signature is detectable although somewhat obscured by later utilitarian development and, sadly, by demolition.

The imaginative plan of the house included a sensuously curved frontage, and for the construction of this Guy Morgan had had a steel 'I'-sectioned girder made and bent to the correct shape. When the bricklayer started to lay bricks upon this he detected a deformation when only two courses were on it. Bringing this to the attention of Miles and the architect, as there were a lot more courses yet to be laid upon it, Guy Morgan refused to believe that such a thing was possible. Miles eventually convinced Morgan that, because of the curvature introduced, the girder was in torsion. He was able to explain this in terms he had previously only employed in designing aircraft and with a few sketches and some mathematics Guy understood what was happening and redesigned the necessary girder.

This house was to become a centre of social activity on such a level as would nearly have satisfied Blossom's Aunt Maxine. There was a fair amount of land surrounding it; the land in that area was particularly cheap at that time as it was prone to flooding and also had a reputation of being the sites of gipsy camps and scrap dealers. Indeed the road leading to it is still called "Beggars Hill Road."

There was a swimming pool, dug single-handedly by the gardener-cum-odd-job man who remained faithful to the family throughout the years to come. This swimming pool was the centre of the weekend gatherings, which often included Blossom's sister Jean and Joan Cliff with her two little boys, Clive and Patrick; Joan Cliff remembers with affection the hospitality and informality of those few sunny days before the storm clouds of war started to appear. Joan recalls one snobbish *grande dame* (was it Maxine, I wonder?) who was 'Lord-and-Ladying' it around and Jean threatened to throw her in the swimming pool if she didn't stop being so superior.

A student of Blossom's, Joan Davis, later Joan Burton, said that Blossom "collected people" and she certainly did. She was in her element: not only did she have the satisfaction of her design work, her interest in the factory and its finances, but she was able to entertain people from the artistic world, and her friends included all the aspects of the arts – at the time she was taking an especial interest in the literary world.

Wargrave-on-Thames was nearby, less than a couple of miles as the crow flies; the River Loddon empties into the Thames at that point, and many of the London society 'upper-crust' had houseboats and summer bungalows there, including the Cliffs. Maidenhead, also not far away, housed the Cliveden set and was notorious as a weekend hideaway especially for those in the theatre. Skindles night-club, Henley regatta, it was all 'go'; famous people, humble aviators, lame ducks, they were all welcome at Lands End House, and if they needed a bed or a job, well, Blossom and Miles would go out of their way to help them.

All this had been made possible by the success of the venture that Charles Powis and Miles had now well established. Three Hawks were under construction by June 1933 and forty employees had been taken on, while a hangar had been ordered and erected in a few weeks. How things progressed at such a fast pace is quite incredible. The hangar was 120 feet long and that was the third hangar erected; with aeroplanes selling at only £450 a time, a workforce of forty and a brand-new home to pay for, it is difficult to see how the books were balanced. Nevertheless progress went on apace with new and exciting projects in the pipeline.

Up until the end of 1934, the maximum production possible was only two aircraft a week, and this was not achieved every week; where was the money coming from? There must be a question whether some of the money involved was Blossom's family money. Her aunt had settled an endowment on her four nieces, and although her aunt was still alive and, indeed, Sir Johnston was still alive, some family money may have been available.

By the end of the trading year for 1934 Phillips & Powis had made a loss of more than £20,000, a large sum at the time. However this was not apparent until the first annual general meeting of the company which did not take place until 1936, so they may have all been living in the proverbial 'fool's paradise' as far as their own perception of the success of the business went.

As far as the mood in 1934 and 1935 was concerned, optimism reigned. The little aircraft attracted so many compliments that more and more hangars were built and a large building to be used in assembling the 'planes was built in front of the hangars; this alone amounted to another 24,000 square feet of factory space.

Only a few months before these expansions, construction of the aircraft had been carried on in a mess of puddles and shavings with a boy with a wheelbarrow carrying components from one work-bench to another, and he had to push this barrow along duckboards to keep out of the muddy water. It was really only old Harry Hull's Draconian discipline that kept any sort of order and efficiency, mainly because he terrified the workers with his glassy stare.

There was a great interest in air racing in those years, and the quest for speed amongst private owners' light aircraft inspired Blossom and Miles to look at the aerodynamic efficiency of their designs. However, you could clean up designs and make them more efficient and therefore faster only up to a point, and then really it was all down to the engine. These days this is obvious but in the days before jet engines were even thought of except in the minds of some very advanced engineers (who were mostly thought of as complete cranks), a larger engine was going to be a gamble, not just in terms of money, but also as to how much a client would be prepared to pay for a faster aircraft.

The first production Hawk, G-ACHJ, was sold to Wing Commander H.M. Probyn and he entered it in the King's Cup Air Race in 1933. Unfortunately he had to make a forced landing with engine trouble, but undaunted as those intrepid lads tended to be, he managed to win the Cinque Ports Wakefield Cup only a fortnight later. The second production Hawk, G-ACKI, also took part in the latter race.

The first variant of the Hawk was the M.2A cabin version and had the more powerful Gipsy III engine; this had been designed by de Havillands specifically for the 'luxurious' aircraft of 1934, fast tourers for the private owner or air taxis. This cabin Hawk was for their old friend and ally of their barnstorming days, Stephen Cliff, who wished to enter it in the Oases Rally in Egypt in January 1934. They did not have to use much ingenuity to register it G-ACLI. Joan Cliff had to go by sea to Egypt as what might have been her space was, of necessity, occupied by extra fuel.

However Joan did get to fly to Budapest and Germany among other places in the 'plane, although she said that she absolutely *hated* flying. There were some advantages for her, though, as she got to meet such famous aviatrixes as Amelia Earheart – at Hamble in 1929. She saw off Elsie McKay, Lord Inchcape's daughter, on her flight from Cranwell to America, who was never to be seen again by anyone. Amy Johnson flew Joan as a passenger from Woodley and Joan remembers that the men (pilots) were "very bitchy" about Amy Johnson and her flying ability though Joan found her flying immaculate.

The Hawk M.2A was later to be completely destroyed by fire while in a hangar at Brooklands. Stephen Cliff was about to sell it, so he had not bothered to renew the insurance for the short time it was there, a matter for regret on two counts.

Meanwhile the excitements of aviation continued to attract the public's interest: not only air racing such as the Mildenhall to Melbourne race, but regular events like Sir Alan Cobham's National Aviation Day which was held every year from 1931, choosing as its location a different major town each year, and others such as the British Hospitals Air Pageant where another of their old friends,

Pauline Gower, gave joyrides to over 10,000 in her three-seater Spartan – two at a time, I hasten to add.

The greatest aerial sporting event was definitely the King's Cup Air Race; this held such prestige for those taking part and sparked the imagination of all and sundry.

Miles had been, strangely for him, reluctant to branch out from his original concept of producing aircraft very cheaply and did not think that there would be a market for faster aircraft which cost more. As all the designs and drawing had hitherto been done by Blossom and himself to a lesser degree, he really did not have that much time to devote to long-term planning of more advanced aircraft. However, one factor that influenced him was the fact that they had used up all the very cheap Cirrus engines that had started him out on his venture.

Recruiting a young draughtsman, Tommy Botting, they decided to produce the Hawk Major. Now this was not too different to look at, as the airframe construction and general aerodynamics of the Hawk had proved too successful to abandon them for a radical new design. The futuristic ideas were to come later. The basic airframe was similar to that of the Hawk, but the wooden engine mounting of the first Hawk Major was replaced on production models with a more conventional metal one. The 130 hp Gipsy Major engine made by de Havillands was an inverted in-line engine and therefore at one stroke improved the lines and the pilot's view. But regardless of these improvements it was still a common sight to see these tail-wheeled aircraft zigzagging crazily from side to side when taxying, the pilot trying to see where he was going, sometimes unsuccessfully with drastic results. Present-day 'taildragger' pilots will understand only too well!

The Hawk Major cost £750, nearly twice as much as Miles' original target price for the Hawk; in spite of this, the first one was sold in July 1934 and by May 1935 seventeen had been made and sixteen sold. G-ACXU finished fifth in the handicapped section of the Mildenhall to Melbourne race in October 1934 and established a single-engined record to Australia.

In the 1934 King's Cup Tommy Rose had come second in the Hawk Major, G-ACTD, which was the prototype aircraft, at a speed of 147 mph; it was to be involved in a fatal crash at Doncaster in

August 1936. H.R.A. Edwards had come sixth in a Martlet and Sir Charles Rose and Miss G. Patterson had taken part in the race in Miles aircraft, the Hawk Speed Six G-ACTE and Hawk G-ACIZ respectively. This might be seen as only moderate success, but by 1935 Miles Aircraft finished first, second, third and fifth, a remarkable achievement by any standards and, most remarkable of all, by such a small company so new on the scene; not only that but a total of thirteen Miles aircraft took part in the 1935 race. The winning speed had by now risen to 176 mph. Miles himself was eleventh in his Sparrowhawk.

To go back to the basic Hawk, which had of course been designed by Blossom, approximately 55 were built, the last in 1934; they included, as well as the M.2A cabin Hawk, the M.2B long-range single-seater which was powered by a Hermes IV engine and had a range of 2,000 miles, and the M.2D which reverted to the Cirrus engine and a range of 450 miles. 1935 seemed to be a bad year for snow as two of the Hawks were destroyed in snowstorms, one in April of that year (in the temperate zone of Royston, Hertfordshire) and one in December when, with the pilot blinded by the snow, it hit a tree in Meir. Unfortunately no Hawks survive today.

Blossom constantly sought to improve the lines of the aircraft, and the Hawk Major, with its clean profile and the undercarriage legs concealed behind streamlined fairings, achieved a top speed of 150 mph. Then, with more experience in the field, they decided to investigate the effect of split flaps. Testing out aluminium flaps fixed to the wings of one of the early Hawks they found such improved characteristics in the coefficient of lift, in the angle of glide and reduction in the landing speed that from then on all Hawk Majors were fitted with split flaps operated by hand by the pilot.

The Hawk Major was to have many variants concluding with the Hawk Trainer. Then came the new Magister, and this was to occupy a very major part of their production. There are several examples still flying today. However speed and beauty was to occupy Blossom's mind and pencil, in particular when Miles gave her a couple of weeks to come up with a design in which he could win the King's Cup. Was he joking? Well, if he was, she rose to the challenge.

*   *   *

The success that Phillips & Powis and Miles had had in these and similar races prompted the formation of the firm as a limited company.

Such a multiplicity of aircraft, variants and modifications erupted from Blossom's intellect; these are well documented in any standard work on aircraft, so I will not explore them in detail here, but some examples have interest apart from the technical data, therefore well worth considering further.

The theme of birds of prey, in particular raptors, continued in the prewar years except for aircraft like the Whitney Straight, which was made for and named after the famous racing driver. There is an elegantly posed sepia photograph of Blossom ostensibly painting a hawk on the fuselage of an aircraft whilst her sister Jean sits with a falcon on her wrist, to be used as a model. When they ran out of birds they used suitable 'M's, Monarch (butterflies again?), Mentor, Monitor and so on.

After the Hawk and Hawk Major, we come to the Hawk Speed Six; only three of these were built. The first was for Sir Charles Rose to fly in the 1934 King's Cup, while the second and third, which were not finished until a year later, were built for a brother and sister, Luis and Ruth Fontes, who also wanted them specifically to enter in the King's Cup of 1935. They did not finish among the winners but in the 1936 King's Cup two of the three finished second and fifth, though not flown by the Fontes that year. Tommy Rose finished second in G-ADOD and he was to become a very famous test pilot, racer and *bon viveur*. He did have the advantage of a 'souped-up' engine, the high compression Gipsy Six R. This aircraft was also entered for the England to Johannesburg Race which took place in September 1936 not long after the King's Cup. This time it was piloted by Flight Lieutenant A.E. Clouston and force-landed in Southern Rhodesia; that was the end of that one.

At the same time that Blossom and Miles were producing the Hawk Major and Speed Six they were developing an aircraft with a proper cabin as opposed to the previous ones which, if they did have any protection for the pilot, just had a cockpit covered by a rudimentary canopy, which of course was cramped and only suitable for racing or real enthusiasts. This new 'plane was called the Falcon, and the production version the Falcon Major. Although a cabin aircraft, this was designed especially for H.L. Brooks to participate in the England to Australia Race in 1934. It made its first flight on October 12th 1934 flown by Miles, of course just in the nick of time. A strange (or typical) constituent of this one was the engine installed, a Gipsy Major, which had previously powered the Puss Moth previously flown across the Atlantic by Jim Mollison. By having the cabin they did not lose too much efficiency, it was only 5 mph slower than the Hawk Major though with a slightly longer take-off.

Twenty Falcon Majors were built, including one for ground instruction and one which suffered an extremely bizarre fate. During the 1937 King's Cup Race it had to make a very sharp turn and experienced such violent turbulence around Scarborough Castle that the two pilots, W/Cs Hilton and Sherron, were thrown clean through the roof of the cabin. A newspaper photographer captured this exact moment, showing the two men in the air above the 'plane. One would imagine that both perished instantly.

The Falcon was then fitted with the 200 hp Gipsy Six engine to make the Falcon Six, in which Tommy Rose scored the highest achievment in the 1935 King's Cup. The Falcon provoked another strange tale during the Spanish Civil War. Three German Stuka dive-bombers were on their way to wreak some havoc during this conflict when they happened to be in the same air space as a Falcon which had been bought by a Spaniard and was being delivered. They had seen nothing like this Falcon in their lives, thought that the Falcon was some new fighter and turned tail and fled.

To return to the King's Cup races, a total of 17 Falcon Sixes were built. The Falcon Six which won the 1935 King's Cup, G-ADLC, was a four-seater, as was the one which took fifth place. Second and third were two Hawk Trainers. G-ADLC beat Amy Johnson's record to Cape Town in February 1936 and then established another record on the return journey.

All these successes, although they may look rather boring on paper when laid out end to end, show without doubt just how skillful Blossom was at designing, but not only that, how well she managed to combine work with the finesse needed to impress prospective clients – what we might call marketing now, but rather more than that because the aviation scene was one of close-knit contacts and delicate negotiations. I am not saying the Miles and the others did not also have big parts to play, but Blossom was the one who held it all together.

Phillips & Powis was by then second only to de Havilland as a producer of light aircraft and when the company was floated as a public company Charles Powis was made Managing Director with Miles as Technical Director; the Company name was changed to Miles Aircraft Limited in October 1943, and the name Miles is now so much more famous and well-remembered than the names of Phillips & Powis.

The next notable aircraft was the Sparrowhawk. Miles wanted desperately to win the King's Cup himself, so he gave Blossom the task of producing an aircraft in which he could achieve his ambition. As stated before there were only a few short weeks to go before the race and there was no production space available, let alone any other facilities. There were twelve other aircraft at Woodley already which were specifically being prepared for the race at this same time, so it looked like an impossible scenario.

Blossom started on the drawings; realistically she knew that there was no chance of producing a 'plane from scratch in the time so she drew a conversion which involved an ordinary Hawk fuselage. This she shortened by 12 inches. She made it more streamlined by lowering the upper structure; this certainly made it more streamlined but it meant that there would be no room for the pilot. As it was only Miles and as he was giving her this Herculean task – well, she laughed, he could sit on the floor! He would have to put his legs over the front spar. She then reduced the span by a hefty 5 feet; now this could not be done aerodynamically simply by chopping bits off the ends of the wings, so the width of the centre section was reduced to just that of the fuselage. The height of the undercarriage had to be reduced to get less drag and the undercarriage itself also had to be moved outwards to get the legs out of the slipstream of the propeller. The problem of several refuelling stops was solved by installing three tanks, one in each wing and one in the fuselage behind the engine. The first day's course was 953 miles and these tanks made it possible for the Sparrowhawk to complete the course with only one stop.

The race was flown in two stages, the first being a more or less complete circuit of Britain starting at Hatfield. This stage was not handicapped, but there were compulsory checking-in points (where you *had* to land) in Scotland, Northern Ireland and Wales. Miles refuelled only in Belfast. He was second when he got to Glasgow, still second when he got to Cardiff and he had really high hopes that he could improve on this and win it: no one was more determined and dedicated, it seemed as if his whole future depended on it. The second stage *was* handicapped and the mysteries of this system were such that, although he did the seven laps of 50 miles each at a mean speed of over 172 mph he was not officially placed. This was a blow to him, having suffered the discomfort of the modified aircraft and flying it at its very limit for hour after hour. It was some consolation to him to find that Tommy Rose had been placed first and then to find out that the second, third and fifth places had been awarded to Miles aircraft, but he still wished that he could have actually seen Tommy gaining first position.

In the 1936 King's Cup the Sparrowhawk was placed ninth, and in the 1937 race seventh; it was again seventh in 1938 and then went on to compete in the fifties after conversion to the Sparrowjet. There were four other Sparrowhawks built in 1936; these had fuselages designed for them and did not just use the old cut-down Hawk version. Altogether six Sparrowhawks were built including two for research, by Miles and R.A.E. Farnborough.

Whilst all this frantic activity was going on, Miles and Blossom were still finding time to devote to research, but in 1936 George Miles and Don Brown joined the firm, George having wound up his buasiness at Shoreham, as recounted earlier. These arrivals roughly coincided with Phillips & Powis going public.

We should really start calling Miles "F.G." now because that is how he was universally known from then onwards. Presumably it avoided confusion now that George was included in the team, but I think it happened spontaneously as Miles was now established as a businessman in the business world and "F.G." had that sort of ring to it.

Actually we can't tie in the birth of the research with George's arrival because as early as 1935, F.G. had a relationship with the

Royal Aeronautical Establishment at Farnborough and they cooperated with each other in some very interesting research projects. So many of these projects were prefaced by the introduction: "This modification was tested and flown in . . . by F.G. Miles on . . . " The first flight of the Hawcon, for instance, took place on November 29th 1935. He had had to design, build and fly the 'plane by then!

*   *   *

It might be fairly obvious from what we have already laid out regarding Blossom's disposition that her political sympathies would be to the left of centre. Her interest in the welfare of her workers might be accepted as customary today but in those days it was quite unusual.

When the Spanish Civil War loomed, many of the intelligentsia of the British Isles had a great deal of affinity for the republican cause. In fact quite a few of our best literary young men sacrificed their lives to this ideal.

For the first time since the first World War aircraft were perceived as strategic weapons. The Spanish Civil War was unusual in the fact that the 'rebels' led by Franco were in fact the fascists and the established (although shaky) government was the Popular Front, comprising Republicans allied to Communism.

Franco had only managed to get about a hundred out-of-date aircraft, so he enlisted the help of Hitler and also Mussolini and therefore obtained some reasonably modern 'planes like Stuka dive bombers, but not very many. So he was in the market for practically anything that was airworthy, and he had the money available.

Great Britain did not want to take sides (or at any rate did not want to be *seen* to take sides), so there were a lot of undercover arms deals taking place, either for money or for ideologies or for both.

Before the war, two Hawk Majors and a Falcon Major were exported to Spain. Then a further four Hawk Majors, a Falcon Six and a Hawk Speed Six were illegally exported to both sides by some rather devious characters. Blossom had absolutely nothing at all to do with these nefarious activities. A few of the aircraft survived; one, a Falcon Six, was returned to the UK and restored to flying condition before returning to Spain by air in 1997.

We can only speculate as to *exactly* where Blossom's political leanings lay and how far their influence extended. However it is on record that several years later the father of one of the girl students at her technical school took his daughter away in high dudgeon as "they're all a lot of Communists there!" His daughter had already been there for some while before this occurrence, so she had had the benefit of the ambience of the school and its education.

It was somewhat extreme to label them "Communists"; the atmosphere of democracy that pervaded the plant was an amalgam of Blossom's intellectualism and artistic family liberalism coupled with F.G.'s hard-working background, pulling himself up by sheer determination. It could have been an uneasy mixture, but the fact was that it worked. It worked not only to their own benefit but to the benefit of everyone who ever had anything to do with them. Their friendship with the extremist politician, Ian Mikado, who was M.P. for Reading, may have been pragmatic.

Blossom's brother-in-law, André Van Gyseghem, was labelled as "a pro-Soviet activist involved with the working-class Unity Theatre" in the thirties but by 1977 his politics must have been more moderate because by then he was living in New York and he described his hobby as "piloting an aeroplane."

*   *   *

One project that contributed towards the future of the company was the Hawcon mentioned earlier; initially this had been a research project to test the effects of varying thicknesses of wings. The Royal Aircraft Establishment had been very interested in this ever since the introduction of monoplanes had meant that wings could no longer be supported, strengthened or braced by wires or struts. The interest, investigation and study of aspects of structures and aerodynamics was mutually satisfying for both parties but it had another very significant point, which was that Phillips & Powis had a very lucrative contract with the R.A.E.

This source of income underpinned the finances of the company and at the same time allowed Blossom and F.G. to indulge their wildest futuristic ideas and designs. A Falcon Six was tested with tapered wings; variable pitch propellers were about to come on the scene; a Sparrowhawk was employed to investigate flaps to give a higher lift when needed at landing and take-off; retractable flaps, thin wings, long wings; the list goes on and on and nearly every one of these experiments has a direct bearing on the airliners we fly in today.

Charles Lindbergh had become one of the most famous men in the world when he flew the Atlantic single-handed in 1927. He was a very handsome man, and "a quiet hero" was how he was described. He was certainly the most famous man in the United States, having only a few hours before the Atlantic feat set a trans-America record; he remains famous today, and when he wrote *"The Spirit of St. Louis"* it won the Pulitzer Prize in 1953. His young son had been kidnapped for ransom and was later murdered, and this added to the general awareness of his fame. The prestige with which he endowed the Miles Company when he commissioned an aircraft to be built especially for him can hardly be imagined under the vast media coverage which is common today. This was the Mohawk, which still exists and is presently being restored to static display condition in the USA.

Lindbergh wanted a comfortable little 'plane which would be fast and with sufficient range that he could tour round Europe on business, taking his wife with him. Powered by the 200 hp American Menasco Buccaneer engine, over which Miles was negotiating with a view to building it under licence, this gave the Mohawk a maximum speed of 185 mph and a range of 1,400 miles.

Lindbergh, who at that time seemed to call F.G. "Freddy," impressed F.G. very much. Apparently he was the perfect person to work for. F.G. said that he spent a good deal of time with him and he knew exactly what he wanted in a 'plane and just how feasible it was to construct the craft according to his criteria. Then F.G. said something very illuminating in the context not only of this particular aircraft but of every one of Miles designs: he said "He knew as well as I did the sort of compromises one has to accept when designing and making an aeroplane," not something that would be accepted today – or not acknowledged, anyway.

They intended to build another Mohawk as it was such a success, but the components made for it were eventually incorporated in a modification called the Nighthawk.

The Mohawk was impressed into military service in 1941 and was used for communications duties with the R.A.F. In 1950 it was sold in Spain, where it was allowed to become derelict. Later rescued, it was taken to the USA for restoration work to be carried out, as mentioned a moment ago.

In spite of all this activity the company again made a loss in the 1937 trading figures. This time it was more than £19,000. The mood amongst Blossom and the team must have still been high because all sorts of activities not directly related to earning any money for the firm were put into practice. Apprenticeship schemes and publication of 'in-house' magazines took up a great deal of Blossom's time.

In 1936 Rolls Royce had purchased a majority holding of the new shares which had been issued, so now the company had a backer with an interest in sustaining the company. The reasons for this purchase were not entirely altruistic as Rolls Royce saw a market for their engines and they also foresaw something that had already occurred to the redoubtable Aunt Maxine.

F.G. suggested to Aunt Maxine, whom he knew had a great deal of money and liked to make more, that Rolls Royce shares would be an excellent investment now that they were increasing their investment in the aero-engine business. I can't think that he saw this as insider trading, but he genuinely believed that this expansion would lead to vast profits. Maxine, however, who was by that time living in her fairyland palace, the Château de l'Horizon on the French Riviera, shook her head.

She said: "I think war is coming. Assets in England will be frozen the moment it comes. I would have to keep my money in America."

Strange how shrewd one elderly actress could be.

Her shrewdness might have been in part associated with her friendship with Winston Churchill. Just how far this friendship went is hard to say; he certainly stayed at the Château on many occasions, but this is when they were both well into 'maturity.' One of his most famous paintings is of the Château. As outlined previously they had known each other since 1911 and Elizabeth von Arnhim (Elizabeth, Countess Russell) was in no doubt about the relationship when she referred to "Maxine Elliot, the mistress of Winston Churchill." *He* was certainly shrewd enough to advise her on international affairs.

Nevertheless, F.G. also thought that a war, at least in Europe, was highly likely and his opinions led him to believe just the opposite of Maxine's conclusions. He thought that the market for military aircraft (which would all need engines) was going to explode – which it did in more senses than one.

It is significant that of the two people who had the most influence on Blossom, their conclusions based on the same facts should be completely and diametrically opposed. It once again illustrates the opposite ends of the spectrum which when welded together in their marriage was to prove so complete.

Charles Powis resigned from the company in 1937. A combination of personal and business reasons probably prompted his resignation, as there does not seem to be any real rift with F.G.; Charles and Pauline Powis had lost a tiny baby with bronchitis and the general direction of the firm and its higher levels of technology probably added up to too much pressure at that point. This meant that the old pioneering days faded into obscurity and the age of advanced mathematical thinking had begun.

*   *   *

Blossom now began to concentrate on the factors which most interested her. Improving the working conditions and the health of her employees held a high priority for her, mind as well as body. This was now a considerable undertaking as, with a contract for Hawk Trainers for the Reserve Training School at Woodley which was to become No.8 Elementary & Reserve Flying Training School, the workforce had now risen to eight hundred! The infrastructure of feeding, paying and instructing these new workers occupied many sessions, but the ultimate total loyalty of all their workforce, present and future, illustrates just how well they set about it.

What were, at the time, ultra-modern methods of stock control and recording transactions (internal and external) were put into effect. Organisation that is taken for granted now was improvised and implemented, all this, as was usual with F.G. and Blossom, done in double-quick time. With hindsight, one might say that all this was because of the apprehension of the imminence of war, but of those in high governmental and commercial positions totally refuted this idea.

Several literary publications were also in Blossom's mind and by 1938 they were put into practice.

*   *   *

Blossom's father, Johnston Forbes-Robertson, had died in retirement on the 6th November 1937 at St. Margarets Bay, Dover, Kent after a long and serious illness. Although he had been retired for a whole generation his obituary in *"The Times"* ran to a full column and a half. The headline was "Beauty and Grace in Acting." This spelled out his career in detail and said that "the quality of his acting was, first and last, beauty," and that he was "a member on the Advisory Committee on Spoken English set up by the B.B.C." An old friend, "A.E.," wrote that he "would remain the vision of a gallant, courteous and comely gentleman" and that in fifty years of friendship "he showed how alluring the art of living may be. The love from his family, the devotion of his friends – his magnetism, those handsome features and high-bred beauty, kindliness, understanding, charity . . . and nothing but generous praise for his contemporaries." He finishes with an eulogy to his "devoted and talented wife and daughters." When his will was published it showed that Johnston had left the sum of £8,372, which, of course, represented a decent sum then but paled into insignificance when compared with his sister-in-law's millions. In his eighty-fifth year his death was not a tragedy but somehow Blossom felt it was a fulfillment, and this prompted her to spend more time and thought on the more cerebral side of the business.

Bearing in mind that they had a little boy, Jeremy John, who was then five years old, there was plenty for Blossom to do but she took on more and more responsibilty for the welfare of the workforce. Of course Jeremy had a devoted nanny, Nanny Hanson; she was a "Norlands Nanny," trained at the prestigious college near Newbury, and she remained close to the family until she died in her eighties. But as Joan Cliff said: "This was not an indulgence." It was entirely the usual practice in that way of life, and as such would not have been a matter for comment or even notice and therefore the perfectly natural way of going about bringing up one's children. Jeremy remembers Lands End House as always being full of "people coming and going."

TOP: Blossom's maternal grandparents, Adelaide Hall Dermot (LEFT) and Captain Thomas Dermot (RIGHT).
BOTTOM: Blossom's parents, Gertrude Elliot (LEFT) and Johnston Forbes-Robertson (RIGHT).
Photos: via Diana Forbes-Robertson.

TOP: Blossom's aunt Maxine (after whom she was named), who exerted such a great influence on her life.
BOTTOM: Aunt Maxine at Marienbad in 1909 with King Edward VII and his party.
Photos: via Diana Forbes-Robertson.

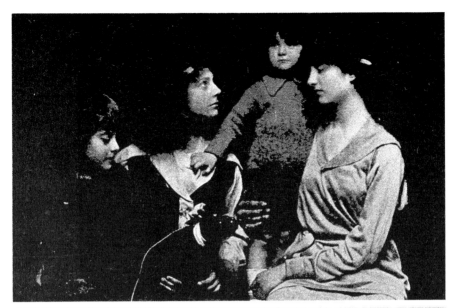

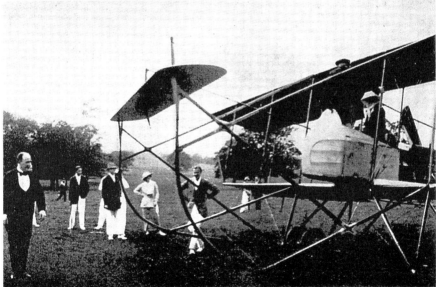

TOP: Maxine's four daughters. L. to R.: Jean, Chloe, Diana (Dinah) and Blossom.
BOTTOM: Claude Grahame-White has just landed his aircraft on aunt Maxine's lawn and is greeted by Dalton the butler.
Photos: via Diana Forbes-Robertson.

CONTRASTS IN THE BACKGROUNDS OF THE EARLY LIVES OF BLOSSOM AND FRED (F.G.) MILES:
TOP: Le Château de l'Horizon in the south of France, one of the palatial homes belonging to Blossom's aunt Maxine. Photo: *"Wide World."*
BOTTOM: The limited facilities of the workshop in which F.G. constructed the "Gnat." Photo: via the Museum of Berkshire Aviation Trustees.

TOP: The aircraft which brought Blossom and F.G. together, the DH.60X
Moth G-EBZG. Photo: The A.J. Jackson Collection.
BOTTOM: Blossom sits in the cockpit of the prototype Miles Hawk, with F.G.
and Charles Powis alongside. Photo: *"Sphere"* of 22nd July 1933 via Peter
Amos.

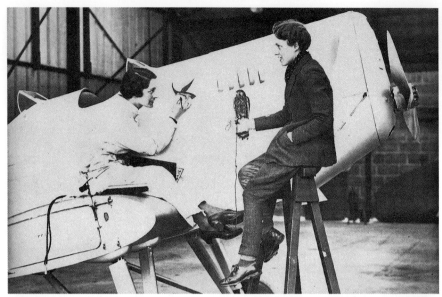

TOP: Blossom paints a hawk motif on the Miles Hawk while her sister Jean holds the 'model' on her wrist. Photo: British Aviation Pictures via Adwest Archives.

BOTTOM: Reading Aero Club personalities pictured in 1938 with a Hawk Trainer in front of the Falcon Hotel at Woodley. L. to R.: Pauline Powis, Ranald Porteous, Firola Fitzgerald, Blossom Miles, Tommy Rose, Diana James. Photo: *"Flying"* via Adwest Archives.

TOP: Stephen Cliff's Hawk M.2A (the only one built), which he flew to Egypt on the Oasis Rally. Photo: Clive Cliff.
BOTTOM: The prototype Hawk M.2D, built in 1934. Photo: via Adwest Archives.

TOP: Blossom starts work on a new design. Photo: Miles Magazine Vol.1, No.2, February 1938.
BOTTOM: "I think that's the best place for it, don't you?" Blossom discusses a cockpit layout with two of the staff. Photo: via Richard Riding.

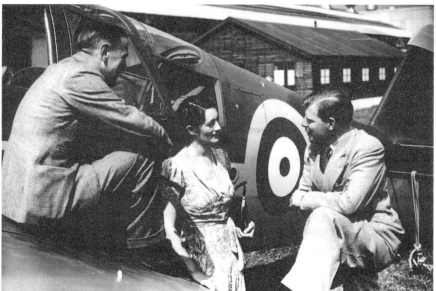

TOP: Blossom, F.G. and son Jeremy pose in front of the diminutive Miles Hobby at an air display in 1938.
BOTTOM: A Miles Master supports Bill Skinner, who is in discussion with Blossom and F.G.
Photos: via Adwest Archives.

CANDID CAMERA!
TOP: "Tarts and Tramps" party at the factory during WW II. Blossom is dressed as a man (2nd from R., front row), while F.G. appears as an old woman (extreme R., front row). Photo: British Aviation Pictures via the Museum of Berkshire Aviation Trustees.
BOTTOM: Blossom in relaxed mood at the fitting shop New Year party on January 1st 1944. Photo: via the Museum of Berkshire Aviation Trustees.

THE MILES AERONAUTICAL TECHNICAL SCHOOL:
TOP: Students in the laboratory with smoke tunnel and other equipment made by themselves.
BOTTOM: Student's Council with tutor Alan Pepper (3rd from left).
Photos: Miles Aeronautical Technical School.

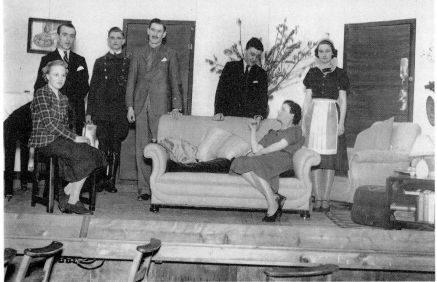

BLOSSOM'S THEATRICAL LEGACY:
TOP: *"Workers' Playtime"* was recorded in the factory. The impressionist Felix Bowness (a Miles employee) is immediately to the left of compère Brian Johnson (holding script).
BOTTOM: Blossom encouraged amateur dramatics; here the "Aerodrome Players" are seen on stage.
Photos: via the Museum of Berkshire Aviation Trustees.

MILES
MAGAZINE

NEWS

WAR
SUPPLEMENT

PRICE 1d. (Entire proceeds go to our charity fund)   Volume 4, No. 8   *Third Anniversary Issue*

MILES AIRCRAFT LIMITED
READING - BERKSHIRE

May 25ᵗʰ 1945

Dear Readers,

Our third anniversary! How I wish we could have a lovely cake with three candles on it and a slice for all our readers, including the boys still serving with the forces.

Since our last number the longed-for news of the end of the European war has come. It won't make much difference to our every day life for some time to come, but what a lovely relief to our spirits! What seems like aeons ago I imagined myself on VE day doing this → while in point of fact this is what I really did →

And I'll bet most people felt the same way. I know it's the best rest I've had for five years, just because it was a real rest with no feeling of "I ought really to be doing some work".

I hope and believe that by next year's anniversary our men will be pouring back from the East, having finished the Japs as completely as they have finished the Nazis.

And I hope that when real peace comes we shall all be together again with more work to do than we know how to cope with!!

My love to you all, here and away.

Maxine Miles —

This front page of Miles "*News*" in 1945 is in Blossom's handwriting.
Photo: via the Museum of Berkshire Aviation Trustees.

Miles Aircraft 1942 — 1947 Works Magazine

NEWS

May 25   one penny

FIFTH ANNIVERSARY

Volume 6   Number 4

A few weeks ago J. J. White came to your editor and said that as May 25th was our 5th anniversary he would like a nice piece for the front page. Your editor said that was splendid and she would let him have it in good time. Everybody knows the way days slip by when you have plenty of time to do a job, so here we are, with a few days to run and no "nice piece" for the front page !

The editor - (I can't go on in the third person) - I am now faced with the problem of what to say. I thought I could start off as they do in pantomime, with

"HERE WE ARE AGAIN"
or,
perhaps more realistically
"HERE WE ARE, STILL GOING STRONG"

Never mind. We are still here and after five years' experience feel up to tackling even an earthquake!

Joking apart, it has not been an easy five years for the people who produce this little paper, and I want once again to thank them on my and your behalf for their successful efforts.

When we started this paper it was published once a fortnight. Then came the Wall Newspaper which was published more frequently, so about a year ago we decided to make the NEWS a monthly magazine and increase its size to 8 pages. We are glad to say that our sales have kept up so we hope this means that you still approve of us.

Now comes the hard part of finishing this article. I can think of no fine peroration so I shall end this as I always ended my letters home from school. "I have no more to say now, so lots and lots of love to all". MAXINE MILES

The Miles "*News*" moved on into the postwar era. In 1947 Blossom's sketches enliven her Editorial.
Photo: via the Museum of Berkshire Aviation Trustees.

LAND'S END HOUSE, TWYFORD, PLAYED AN IMPORTANT PART IN
BLOSSOM'S LIFE IN THE THIRTIES AND FORTIES:
TOP: An aerial view of Land's End house. Photo: via the Museum of Berkshire
Aviation Trustees.
BOTTOM LEFT AND RIGHT: Two interior views reveal the modernistic
styling. Photos: via Jean Fostekew.

MORE HOUSES WHICH MEANT A LOT TO BLOSSOM:
TOP: The gardens of Bedford Square, where she played in childhood (LEFT).
The house at 22 Bedford Square, London, where she grew up (RIGHT).
Photos: Jean Fostekew.
BOTTOM: Batts in Ashurst, Sussex, her last home. Photo: David Russell.

In 1938 the publication of the *"Miles Magazines"* began, to be followed later by the *"Miles Works Magazines"* and then a literary publication called *"Kite."* The latter were inspired by, and in most cases largely edited and partly written by, Blossom. It is interesting that although, as we have seen, the firm was still called Phillips & Powis, the magazines were entitled with the Miles name. There were just a few of the oldest original workers who implied that they thought the Miles were "upstarts" and liked to hark back to the days of working under Mr Powis. Sometimes these traditionally-minded carpenters and craftsmen grumbled that Miles took on too many projects and that they would be better served to concentrate on fewer products, but most of the younger employees were proud to be involved in such a forward-looking firm and excited by the prospect of futuristic, science-fiction types of experimental aircraft. In a way they were both right.

The first edition of the *"Miles Magazine"* was published in January 1938. This was actually edited by A.H. Lukins who was to edit the more technical books like *"Miles Aircraft"* published by Harborough after the war, but Blossom's influence can be seen especially in an article in it which says:

"Mrs Miles designed the Sparrowhawk particularly for Mr Miles' personal use. This little job is absolutely delightful to fly and was thoroughly successful but Mr Miles wanted to go one step further. So in January 1937 he decided to build a fast little machine for the King's Cup Race. It was to have a top speed of something over 200 mph, a Series II Gipsy Major engine, and to incorporate all the fine qualities of the Sparrowhawk with the additional comfort provided by a coupé top.

Then Mr Miles, Mrs Miles and their personal staff got down to the job in their spare time, and it was not long before the basic design was available. It was very difficult to decide what to call this little machine. The smallest of the Hawk class and promising to look very pretty, it was to be made for Mr Miles personally, and his hobby, of course, is – aeroplanes.

Now came the quest of a name for the new model. After dinner one night a conference was held. Reference books were consulted and rejected. Then from Mr Miles, who was looking at a book on falconry, came a roar of laughter. "What's the joke?" we asked. He told us that he had just read about a hawk that was so small that it could only eat butterflies and was inclined to fly into such tempers that it choked itself.

"It's called the Hobby," he said.

That of course was the name we wanted. Except for the bad temper it fitted in everywhere and was a perfect description of the new racing 'plane. So the "Hobby" it became.

Two young men worked on the building of the aircraft – Brian Swann did the metal work and Jack Sullivan did the woodwork, but about six weeks before the King's Cup it looked as if we should not succeed in finishing the aeroplane in time so we got quite a gang of assistants to help. Working day and night this bunch of young enthusiasts rushed the job through under the design supervision of Tommy Botting.

We had just one week left before the Certificate of Airworthiness had to be obtained. Could it be done? They had plenty of bad luck. It was found that the undercarriage was not up to strength, for example, so rapid modifications were put through. Last of all, great difficulty was encountered in making satisfactory undercarriage fairings.

One day left! The fellows had been working sleepless day and night for at least three days and just could not carry on any more – but unless they did carry on the undercarriage fairing would not be done. The aircraft flew that day without its fairings; it was fast, satisfactory, and very comfortable.

The fairings were not done and the machine was not sent to Martlesham, so it could not be flown in the King's Cup. Bad luck! However the "Hobby" is not out of things. Just keep your eye on it in future races – you will see what she can do then."

The above article is not signed but there is no doubt in my mind that it was written by Blossom. The stilted "Mr & Mrs Miles," the impeccable grammar, the intimate details, the incurable optimism, her style exactly.

It would be interesting to find out which bird book F.G. was reading that gave information such as Hobbies losing their tempers!

This article is all the more puzzling when one reads what was written about the Hobby by Lukins himself at a later date. He says:

"It is the policy of Miles Aircraft Organisation to prove their theories by practical tests, rather than to arrive at conclusions on paper and then let matters take their course. After all, it is much more profitable to be able to tell a prospective customer that you KNOW a design is good rather than have to tell him that you BELIEVE it to be so. In pursuance of this policy the thirteenth Miles basic design was intended, primarily, to serve as a flying scale research model to test certain aerodynamic theories and, secondly, to be flown by Mr Miles in the 1937 King's Cup Air Race.

Known as the Hobby, this diminutive low-wing coupé mono-plane had a span of 21 ft 5 ins. and a wing area of only 78 sq ft – less than half the wing area of the celebrated Hawk!

Although the machine was present at Hatfield on the day of the race, last-minute difficulties with its retracting under-carriage had prevented its completion in time to qualify as a competitor, much to the disappointment of Mr Miles.

However, after the completion of the intended experiments, the machine was purchased by the Royal Aircraft Establish-ment, Farnborough, as the small dimensions permitted its use in the large wind tunnel there. Considerable information of the utmost importance was gained from the Farnborough tests, tests made doubly useful by the fact that the results could be cross-checked by actual flight trials."

One might think that this report on the Hobby conflicts with Blossom's account of the 'plane and its gestation. Blossom and Fred were nothing if not ingenious at turning adversity into advantage. Obviously they could think of several good uses for any one design; their good relations with the Farnborough boffins stood them in good stead not only on this occasion.

The differences also illustrate how publicity and public relations had begun to be recognised and set out in commercial literature in the intervening years. It would not do to emphasise the ad hoc, happy-go-lucky enthusiasm of prewar days when hoping to make an impression on prospective customers.

Regarding "Mr Miles' hobbies," given in the first article as "of course – aeroplanes," in an article in another magazine he is described as "an enthusiast on cinematography and a keen yachtsman, but he rarely has time for either hobby." This same potted biography refers to him as being "conversant with all aspects of factory life, having run the gamut from flying, through making, to designing aircraft. . . . The spirit of enthusiasm and creative effort, so evident in the Miles Organisation, can be attributed to his outstanding personality." No, I don't think Blossom wrote that one! It is not that she would not have agreed with it, but I think she would have to have been a *bit* more modest, and anyway, it is not in her style.

These first *"Miles Magazines"* were priced at sixpence, carried advertisements and were aimed more at potential customers than at the workforce. A *"Wall Magazine"* was published in the factory; this was Blossom's idea and it was superseded by the *"Miles Works Magazines"* which were first published (at one penny) in 1942. These were edited, illustrated and often mainly written by her.

Then in 1944 she wrote the introduction to a series of three little books called "Milestones":

> "One of the most popular features of the NEWS has been "Milestones," the series of articles by D.L. Brown describing the different types of aircraft designed and built by Miles since he started. As the result of many requests we have decided to reprint these articles in booklet form so that those interested may have a compact and useful record of all Miles types. The first volume runs from the first aeroplane attempted to the M.25. If this booklet meets with success we hope to bring out a second volume.
>
> D.L. Brown has been associated with the building of Miles aeroplanes since the early days of the Gnat and the Martlet. He is now personal assistant to G.H. Miles, Design Director of Miles Aircraft Ltd, so a better chronicler would be hard to find. The money from the sales will be equally divided between the R.A.F. Benevolent Fund and the Miles Trust Fund; so the publication will, I hope, meet the demand of those interested in Miles aeroplanes and help to swell the funds of two deserving causes.
>
> M. Miles."

One can see that her style had changed between 1938 and 1944, it was much less personal and more assured (and less compelling because of this?). One thing that does come through, however, is her concern for the welfare of others. I know nothing about the Miles Trust Fund or whom it was to meant to assist but one of her projects was a Housing Association.

During the war and for a long time afterwards, to obtain any sort of accommodation was so difficult as to be well-nigh impossible. In the light of this Blossom created a Housing Association, one of the many forward-looking and helpful ideas that she had. It was to be set up on very modern and business-like principles but due to unforeseen events it later fell by the wayside.

The architect Guy Morgan, who had designed their house, completed the plans for the Falcon Hotel. This was built by Collier and Catley, a Reading firm, on a slip road jutting right out into the airfield. Because of the prominence of it and its distinctive architecture a lot of people thought that it was the control tower, and many to this day ask: "What happened to the control tower?" and don't really believe it when they are told that it was never a control tower but an hotel. This was quite a famous building in its time, where all the famous aviators and aviatrixes downed quite a lot of alcohol before setting forth in their little craft, not advisable now, but then . . . well, some said they couldn't fly without it!

While Blossom was concentrating on workers' welfare, housing, dramatic societies, literary circles and other schemes to create a small utopia at Woodley, F.G. was expressing his opinions on how *he* thought the progress of the firm should take place. He considered that Phillips & Powis should concentrate on establishing itself as the leading manufacturer of training aircraft (this with any future war in mind) while not relinquishing its already considerable presence in the civil aircraft field, but that, thinking of a commercial empire, they should start building large passenger aircraft and freighters.

Transatlantic airliners, futuristic designs like the 'X' Minor and Major: all these projects were whirring round in F.G.'s head. George and Don Brown were thinking up new ideas by the score, experimental control surfaces, new materials, improvements in engine design: there was no standing still and all the time the news from Europe was getting more and more ominous.

The contrasts between Blossom's and F.G.'s characters and attitudes were shown in stark silhouette by these developments but still they complemented each other and enhanced each other's qualities.

In 1939 their second child was born.

CHAPTER 7

WAR LOOMS: BUSINESS BOOMS

Their daughter, Mary Susannah, was born on June 7th 1939 at 27 Welbeck Street, Marylebone, London, as Jeremy (who was by then six years old) had been. This was in the famous Harley Street area of expensive maternity and medical care. One would have thought that Blossom at the age of thirty-seven, nearly thirty-eight, would begin to take a back seat as far as the firm was concerned.

This does not appear to have happened. Of course the inevitability of war was looming. There was a still a great hope in the country that it could be avoided and I think Blossom held on to this, while F.G. took the opposite view and made preparations commensurate with his ideas. Meanwhile, life had to go on, whatever was expected to happen.

With all the hustle and bustle amongst the varied opinions regarding 'war or no war' in the government and allied civil service bodies, a specification had been drawn up for another basic training aircraft to replace the existing trainers, which were the de Havilland Tiger Moth and the Miles Magister. F.G. always believed that it was a specification impossible to meet. Briefly this aircraft had to meet the requirements of being larger and heavier than the Magister, and was to be a two-seater with a de Havilland Gipsy Six engine. Unbelievably, it was to have open cockpits! It is hard to see what Air Ministry brain thought that this would be an advance on anything at all.

In spite of his doubts, F.G. went ahead with a design. Two aircraft were actually built; the silhouette hardly differed from the standard Hawk/Magister lines, being about five feet longer and only a couple of feet greater in span. Four other firms also put money and effort into this project but none of them made any more impression on the Air Ministry than Miles did, who had wasted valuable time on it. I guess they were all paid some sort of fees for their efforts but it was time that could have been spent to more advantage by all of them.

The prototype M.15, as it was designated, was test-flown in February 1939 by their chief test pilot, Bill Skinner, who was not long afterwards to die of a sub-arachnoid haemorrhage at the tragically early age of thirty-six. Some of the workforce thought that this had been precipitated by his penchant for flying upside down, which he did on every possible occasion and for extended periods. This seems a far-fetched idea, but who knows which is cause and which is effect?

However Magister production was well under way, and many other projects were still on the drawing board and in the pipeline. One great hope of F.G. was for the success of the first Miles twin-engined 'plane, the Peregrine; this had a retractable undercarriage but otherwise looked superficially rather similar to the Percival Q-6. Unfortunately this project coincided with the order for a large number of Magisters, but Don Brown considered that the Peregrine was "the most efficient aeroplane of its class ever built." There were many innovative and exciting features incorporated in this 'plane, and the second one was used for experimental tests in boundary layer control, but when the prospect of war became more apparent, the R.A.F. had to concentrate on quantity rather than quality and the Peregrine was shelved.

War looms – business booms: the two of necessity go together.

There is no doubt that the second World War was responsible for the prosperity of Phillips & Powis/Miles Aircraft, but this was true for most other manufacturers, and not only in the field of aviation. It was their salvation but was also to prove their downfall. However with a new baby, a new house, a new garden, new friends and new responsibilities, Blossom with her usual calm optimism found that life was full and rewarding and exciting.

With uncharacteristic forethought the government of the day had inaugurated the Civil Air Guard scheme on October 1st 1938. This was to provide subsidies for existing flying clubs throughout the country to train pilots. Anyone between eighteen and fifty years of age, provided they were British, could take advantage of this subsidy as long as they were able to pass the medical examination. This applied to *either sex*. The scheme was overseen by five

Commissioners. This was an honorary, unpaid post and I can't imagine that people were tripping over each other to burden themselves with such responsibility. The structure of the five Commissioners was as follows: one had to be Scottish (or at least represent Scotland), two had to represent the Council for Light Aero Clubs, and at least one had to be a woman! The Chief Commissioner was the Right Honourable the Marquis of Londonderry and, of course, they found the statutory woman in Blossom (see Appendix 2 for more details). Now it has always been said that this was a great honour and reflected her status in the world of aviation, but I wonder; Lord Londonderry had to choose someone to represent women pilots and how many did he know?

Whatever the Commissioners thought of the onus of their pressganged task, the response from the general public was immense and incredible. The subsidy of £50 paid to flying clubs for every 'A' licence gained meant that they could offer instruction at five shillings an hour, and ten shillings at weekends. Within the first week no fewer than 16,000 applications had been received and the tempo was kept up throughout the rest of that year and the next. I don't think anyone in authority could have realised that the hunger to fly was so strong.

Naturally these numbers created panic in the administration and the clubs had to call for a temporary halt. It must have been good practice for what was to come. The main criticism from the establishment and the dodos was that it was a waste of money to treat women to the same subsidy as men as they would not be useful if a conflict came. I can imagine that Blossom would try to set that straight, although the attitude to women in any branch of the armed forces is still equivocal and that bias is still current today.

There was also a dog-in-the-manger attitude amongst those who could already fly. It was sheer snobbery really; they didn't like the idea of *their* skies being full of *hoi polloi;* "Is this what we pay our taxes for?" etc. Thus Blossom's new position was an uncomfortable one on several counts. Lady Bailey wrote to the magazine *"The Aeroplane"* defending women pilots and their potential.

C.G. Grey, the editor, replied:

"We quite agree with her that there millions of women in the country who could do useful jobs in the war. But the trouble is that so many of them insist on wanting to do jobs which they are quite incapable of doing. The menace is the woman who thinks she ought to be flying a high-speed bomber when she really has not the intelligence to scrub the floor of a hospital properly, or who wants to nose around as an Air Raid Warden and yet can't cook her husband's dinner."

[He gets a bit nervous here and goes on:]

"There are men like that too, so there is no need to charge us with anti-feminism. One of the most difficult types of men with whom one has to deal is that which has a certain amount of ability, too much self-confidence, an overload of conceit, a dislike of taking orders and not enough experience to balance one against the other by his own will. The combination is perhaps more common among women than men."

[And then he delivers his coup de grace:]

"And it is one of the commonest cause of crashes, in aeroplanes and other ways."

Any woman reading that either in 1939 or today would or will have to take a deep breath here. It more than illustrates what Blossom had to overcome and was still to overcome.

With regard to the dubious honour of being the first woman Commissioner of the Civil Air Guard, the official line is that "Mrs. F.G. Miles retired from the picture to start a family." This is obviously not true because she already had one six-year-old and must have been already pregnant when the job came up; also, knowing her character and determination, I am sure that if she thought the job was worth doing she would have done it, family or no family. Of course a comparatively 'elderly' pregancy is no joke and there may have been pressure from her doctor or from "Freddy" himself, concerned for her welfare. The coincidence is that when she relinquished the post the natural choice for her successor was Pauline Gower, her old mate of the barnstorming days. The tragic irony, too, is that Pauline was to die in childbirth at only 36: Blossom was already 38.

Pauline had to run the gauntlet of male chauvinism, even more so because at that time she was not married. There were letters in the papers and, of course, in *"The Aeroplane"*: "Women should be ashamed of themselves," "disgusting" and so on, those latter remarks being from women correspondents – or so they signed themselves.

In fact the mood regarding women was as questionable as some people's attitude to the coming war. Charles Lindbergh "had enormous admiration for the Germans." John Slessor wrote of him: "I would guess that he was properly sucked in by people like Goering," but so were quite a few of the upper strata of society in England. The only thing that can be said for Lindbergh in the circumstances was that, having been presented by Goering with the Cross of the German Eagle and Star, he never wore it.

From now on we do not see Blossom taking such a direct participation in the designing of aircraft. Miles had recruited teams of scientists – specialist stress office staff, aerodynamicists, researchers – necessary for the large scale projects and production under the leadership of George Miles and Don Brown. F.G. himself no longer did the bulk of the test flying; Bill Skinner was followed by Flight Lieutenant Tommy Rose, assisted by Hugh Kennedy, George and others. In fact it was said that the Air Ministry banned F.G. from flying at all as he was much too important for the war effort.

Walter Capley (said to be "second only to F.G. in his dynamic drive") was Swiss and a very skilful stressman as well as pilot. Capley was later to lose his life when a Spitfire which had just been repaired by the Miles Repair and Service facility lost a wing while landing at Woodley. This was due to the failure of a flawed component and had nothing to do with the Repair and Service department. This was a terrible blow to the company as well as to F.G. and Blossom.

The casual days of "see if it will work" were over, and no one knew better than Blossom that her mathematical, scientific and technical knowledge was naturally limited.

*   *   *

To return to 1939, war eventually came. September saw the first German Stuka dive bombers over England. It is all very well being brave about one's own life, but once one has children, the fear for them and the terror of the unknown is hard to bear. Blossom, in common with the whole population, quietly determined to play a part in defeating an enemy who dared to threaten what was suddenly perceived as an idyllic way of life. She now took on tasks eminently suited to her skills.

With so much of the actual production and business of the firm becoming dependent on wartime commitments and a necessarily rigid administrative structure, it was inevitable that Blossom should not be seen to be taking such a 'hands on' part in designing aircraft and running the factory. However she did instigate a process which was to be vital to the war effort. It was soon apparent in the early days of the war that all able-bodied men were going to be required in the armed forces and all the technical employees who were not absolutely in the forefront of design and development were going to be called up. In fact many of those who *were* in the category of a 'reserved occupation' were desperate to be relieved of this responsiblility and join up, especially in the Royal Air Force. This meant that there was going to be a severe shortage of the middle range of technical staff and of skilled and semi-skilled trades. Blossom was one of the first to recognise this and one of the *very* first to do something about it.

She set up a training scheme for women to participate in engineering draughting. She requisitioned premises in Reading, just inside the borough, so that it was not too far from Woodley and, starting with twenty women, trained female drawing office staff to a high standard. This was really the 'foot-in-the-door' as far as the employment of women in aircraft factories was concerned, and more and more women were taken on in other departments as well as in their traditionally-seen roles of typists and secretaries. The women in the Experimental Department's Liverpool Road drawing office were known rather insultingly as "Blossom's Babies," but as the years went by those who were known by that soubriquet became proud of the fact that they were the first ones and therefore the elite, and they are proud of it to this day; they had an enormous affection for Blossom. Some of them went on to be trained in higher skills and qualified as structural engineers, stresswomen and aerodynamicists.

Other factors started playing their part in her life as well. Domestic staff and the sort of support one could expect from local tradespeople meant that a whole way of life for the strata of society that Blossom had been brought up to take for granted was changing rapidly and actually was never to be in place again.

The onset of food rationing, gas masks, air raid sirens, air raid shelters, no private motoring – all these were shocks for the whole population but especially so for Blossom, a mother of two children, because she wanted to do so many other things rather than just pit her wits against the day-to-day problems of a nation at war.

She saw for the first time that the problems she now faced had been faced by the vast majority of the population all their lives. Now with the workforce in the factory rapidly growing to thousands she saw clearly how she could play her part, not only in the war effort but in alleviating the stresses, mental and physical, which the general public had accepted as normal. Obviously this would not only benefit the people but, by increasing their efficiency and general well-being, would play a vital role in the war effort. Previously her contact with men and women outside her immediate circle might have run into hundreds: now she had thousands upon whom she could bring to bear her influence and idealism.

So she set about some serious thought into how she could help the situation. The first thing that was apparent to her was the generally poor health and physical condition of a lot of the workforce, especially the women. Tuberculosis was still rife among all classes of society – it was incredibly infectious in close communication and a closed atmosphere; malnutrition was not uncommon; pulmonary complaints such as bronchitis were aggravated by the emissions from the coal fires which were the only form of heating most houses had; and pneumonia was usually fatal. It seemed to her that the inactivity of sitting at a desk, bending over a typewriter or drawing board or standing at a workbench or lathe was not good for practically every part of the body.

Blossom instigated series of exercises presided over by qualified instructors, which took place in the workers' lunch breaks. We have films of office workers doing 'physical jerks' in the garden of

Hawkhurst, which was the house next door to the factory. It all looks very much in the tradition of the "Health and Beauty Movement" which was very dear to the heart of the Teutonic races and of Hitler himself, but the healthy, happy faces (specially for the film camera?) of those participating presumably meant that they did not resent too much having to give up their lunch hours!

The film is entitled *"Keeping Fit as an Aid to War Production."* There is no sound-track but it is in colour, which is rather remarkable for the time. The action takes place on a sunny day; the grass looks quite parched, although the colour may not be quite true – nevertheless it seems to have been a dry summer. The opening script is as follows :

> "As an incentive to war production Mrs F.G. Miles, well-known as a designer and a director of Phillips & Powis Aircraft Ltd has inaugurated a series of morning exercises for women of all ages employed in the factory on sedentary work. The classes are under the direction of a qualified instructress and are held twice weekly for a period of thirty minutes."

There follows some simple jigging up and down, dancing round and round and the caption:

> "The following pictures are of pupils undergoing elementary training."

The film continues with a lot of skipping about, until:

> "Then we have the same pupils at a more advanced stage; notice the improved flexibility and control of their muscles and limbs."

This is followed by sequences of rather thin ladies doing a lot of tugging at each others' arms and falling over, evidently exhausted, followed by the words:

> "These exercises have been enthusiastically realized by the employees, who range from single girls to mothers, working on war production and they return to their office, drawing-board and work-bench ready to step up the production of aircraft."

110

There are then more sequences, mainly of dancing in circles, which are completed by the text:

"Arranged in full cooperation with the Council for Recreative Physical Training, this experiment has been a great success."

It is all very well for us to be amused at the unsophisticated approach of this film, but it amounted to a huge leap in the perception of what was to be possible in the education of mind and body. Many, many times Blossom was to demonstrate this perceptive ability.

Her concern for the artistic well-being of the workers was reflected in her support of the Phillips & Powis Players. This was an amateur dramatic society of a high degree of competence.

Blossom's own disability may have prompted her to encourage the employment of blind and disabled personnel. This was quite unprecedented at that time in 1942 when it was intitiated and included some men who had already been blinded in the war. Once again they proved her right in the fact that they could do their jobs efficiently, and the effect on their morale was immeasurable.

It wasn't only on the home and domestic front that shortages made life difficult, but in the factory material shortages were even worse than the shortage of labour; there was not much Blossom could do about this, but it took its toll on F.G., and especially as the taxation laws were already so complex it was hard for him to maintain the sort of equilibrium that Blossom seemed to be capable of; she could diffuse her frustrations in her other activities but it must have been exceptionally wearing for F.G. and his brother George to be working so hard against so many odds, achieving so much and yet still being under the sword of the taxman.

*   *   *

Blossom had a Railton car; it was two-tone blue, dark blue above and a delicate light blue below with a chrome stripe. This Napier Railton was an elegant vehicle, but they also had a fleet of little Fiat 500s, Topolinos, one of which was written off when the headmaster of the Technical School put it into reverse while travelling forward.

During the war when nobody else was allowed to drive except for certain categories like doctors, no doubt Blossom and the associated upper echelons of Phillips & Powis would have had a petrol allowance and permission to use their cars, but to have such a luxurious, thirsty car as the Railton set rather a bad example and she thought that it was seen as an unneccessary extravagance. So for several years she kept it in one of the hangars which was later to become part of the Technical School. Only a few of the students knew of its existence, but one, David Godfrey, remembers seeing the Railton in the dope shop at the factory being resprayed while F.G.'s beautiful mahogany yacht was being overhauled in another workshop.

Although careful in some respects, like not smoking while driving, she nevertheless drove with the 'verve and aplomb' which went naturally with such a vehicle. One day she drove it straight out of the factory gates into the side of a double-decker bus. The Railton, being made of stern stuff, sustained no damage but the side of the bus was severely dented. Blossom, undaunted by the contretemps, took the bus driver inside where she plied him with sandwiches and tea whilst in the factory a few surprised employees replaced the damaged panel and painted it; the bus left on schedule. The outcome might have been tragically different if she had driven the *Fiat* into the bus: no seat belts then.

With all the frantic activity which went with wartime aircraft production, F.G. and George were still engaged in projects of an almost science-fictional nature. They had so many ideas and a lot of these had to be highly secret; some were kept secret even from the Ministry of Aircraft Production itself because, like most government bodies, it had a conservative approach to any new ideas.

Sometime during this period a wind-tunnel was built, concealed in some old farm buildings. It would be nice to think that under today's conservation climate these barns would have been considered 'historic' and hence potential candidates for being registered as listed buildings, but in fact they were knocked down in the recent past during the building of yet another housing estate. They were located at Davis Farm, on the far eastern side of the airfield, well away from the main factory buildings; in fact they were nearer to the Miles' own house than to the factory itself. This wind-tunnel was powered by a Rolls Royce Kestrel engine taken from the Miles M.9 Kestrel prototype. In spite of this, its location and the camouflage provided by the barns was so successful that some folks who worked for two years within fifty yards of it were totally unaware of its existence, and I was one of them.

On the subject of camouflage, the airfield itself was actually camouflaged. Series of wide curved stripes were painted right across the grass of the whole field to represent country lanes and large roundish blobs of green were dotted about to represent trees and shrubs. The undertaking must have been a mammoth task, especially with the shortage of paint and manpower. I can't think that this was one of Blossom's ideas. It seems too bizarre for present-day thought, but then so does the fact that the local Home Guard at the time were issued with one rifle and two bullets to keep the Germans from our shores. First one of the "Dad's Army" carried the rifle and the other the bullets and then they took turns. The country had to do what it could with whatever it had to hand.

Whether the camouflaged airfield ever did fool overhead bombers is doubtful, but certainly there was only really one occasion when it was seriously bombed and this turned out to be by a German pilot who had actually learnt to fly at Woodley, so he knew all the landmarks, rivers, railway lines and so on. Naturally this fact only came to light after the war was over and we were all pals again . . .

In 1940 Phillips & Powis set up a shadow factory at South Marston near Swindon in Wiltshire, where a considerable number of Master IIIs were built. There was also another shadow factory at Doncaster.

The Liverpool Road site where Blossom had started the Drawing Office training scheme was the place where some of the projects that F.G. and George did not want the Ministry to know about were designed and built. One of George's projects, the Libellula canard-wing experimental aircraft, was actually brought from Liverpool Road in the dead of night, to be test-flown by George himself, of course, from Woodley airfield in the very early morning light. The chief test pilot at the time having refused to fly such a strange-looking beast, George was obliged to show his faith in his design by flying it himself, an event which took place not without considerable alarms and excursions, hazardous enough for the test pilot to consider whether he had made the right decision. No experimental or other work on aircraft was supposed to be allowed without express authority from the Air Ministry, but it looks as if in 1942 or thereabouts, Axis spies probably knew more about the Libellula than the British officials.

*   *   *

Meanwhile Blossom was throwing herself into projects aimed to improve the morale of the work force. She still found time to design the costumes for the production of a revival of *"Berkeley Square"* which her sister Jean, who by then had married André Van Gyseghem, was putting on at the Vaudeville. Having such theatrical roots on both sides of her family, Blossom could not but take an interest in her sister's fame and fortune, and to take part in this way was an absolute must for her as wartime propaganda morale-boosters like "Worker's Playtime" also occupied some of her time and efforts. "Worker's Playtime" was a very popular programme on the radio (or "wireless" as it was referred to then). Brian Johnston and other personalities went round to factories, broadcasting from them with standard gags and musical acts, and the applause and roars of laughter and appreciation from the audience seemed out of all proportion to the material itself; however, it was one way of showing Hitler: "Are we downhearted?" "NO . . . OH . . . OH."

*   *   *

In order to explore Blossom's literary contributions to various journals it is perhaps helpful to recap to her first writings and then follow on through the war years. With the initial publication of the *"Miles Magazine"* in January 1938, we can detect the touch of influence of Blossom although no article or editorial is signed. Remember that at that time, and until October 1943, the firm was still really Phillips & Powis; however few referred to them by this name and so perhaps it is not that strange that this publication, and indeed subsequent other news sheets and magazines, were already firmly entitled "Miles."

The *"Miles Magazine"* was quite a tidy little booklet with a semi-stiff cover in colour. It was printed in Torquay and it did say in very small letters at the back that it was indeed published by Phillips & Powis Ltd. However it was obvious that by then the name Miles had achieved an importance outweighing that of Phillips & Powis.

By issue No.3 in March 1938 Blossom's influence is quite clearly seen, reflected in an article by Mrs L.J. Hackett, formerly Elise Battye. This is entitled *"Aventure Française"* and is an extremely amusing account of the women's air race held in in France in 1935 between Paris to Cannes called the "Helene Boucher Cup." Mrs Hackett was an aquaintance of Blossom's from the old days of barnstorming or just after, and in 1934 she possessed an ancient biplane, but when she bought a Hawk Major she thought it "quite the best aeroplane that Mr Miles had ever produced." G-ADLA was entered for the 1935 King's Cup and although Elise was not placed she nevertheless basked in the reflected glory of the success of all the other Miles types.

An article in the same edition is unsigned but do we detect a theatrical turn of phrase? It is entitled *"Birth of an Aeroplane"* with subtitles such as: "A slightly coloured, slightly prejudiced view of the function of the Drawing Office (or D.O.) in the production of a new design." Also included is: "A tame clairvoyant with crystal is a great asset!" We are addressed as "dear reader," and find expressions such as "Oh! no, dearie me" and "But actually it is an awfully decent life if you like that sort of thing – and we do." These have a very feminine, girl's school, melodramatic ring to them.

There is even poetry, a poem called *"Aeronautics From Within,"* subtitled *"The Designer"* and signed at the end "WB." Part of this may be worth repeating to give us a clue as to who "WB" might be.

"Behold an Aeroplane Designer
Envisioning a new Air Liner.
We see him now, the lucky man,
Reclined at ease on a divan.

But when the summer sun declines
And pilots meet to shoot their lines,
When secretaries shelve their files
And pay to watch Clark Gable's smiles,
When departmental heads depart
To pubs to throw a nimble dart,
Or to a Milk Bar, if they're meeker,
He suddenly shouts out "Eureka!"

With this odd trifle off his chest,
He can afford to take a rest,
So settling in to calm repose,
He lets his weary eyelids close.
Lulled by a joss-stick's soft aroma
He slowly falls into a coma,
While singers chant (or that's my story)
Arias from "Il Trovatore."
Let's leave him there – what could be finer
Than being an Aircraft Designer?"

Who else could have written this in 1938? We will never know for sure but the references are interesting: "Il Trovatore," "joss-stick's soft aroma," "Clark Gable's smiles" and the seeming intimate relationship with the "Designer."

Although I do not think that anyone would consider F.G.'s features to be conventionally handsome, there was a certain likeness to Clark Gable and also of Clark Gable to Tony Wilding, Blossom's childhood hero.

"WB": could it stand for "Wife Blossom"?

In the first issue there is a full-page photograph which is labelled: "A Pleasing Study of Mr and Mrs F.G. Miles." It is indeed a pleasing study, lit by natural light; they are looking out of a large window, presumably in the drawing office because a vague outline of an aircraft is seen outside. Once again Blossom is in profile and they are both looking exceedingly happy as they probably had every reason to be in January 1938.

Later editions of the various publications, *"Miles Magazine,"* *"Miles Magazine News,"* *"Wartime Supplement"* and, later, *"Kite"* and *"Milestones"* have signed contributions both from Blossom and F.G. and also a lot of sketches accompanying Blossom's articles, so we can recognise her sketches and illustrations whether signed or not. There are also examples of her handwriting.

The Christmas 1938 *"Miles Magazine"* is a very light-hearted issue with even a colour centrefold of two aircraft, a Kestrel and the prototype Monarch, signed "Morton," but this is the name of the printer (C. & C. Morton, Bembridge, I.O.W.), not the artist. One of the stories is an account of Christmas shopping with a small boy buying presents for Daddy and Nanny, all aviation-related gifts.

The sketches accompanying this are signed with a stylised "T" with a dot on either side loosely resembling an aircraft. They depict, amongst toys and shoppers, an elegant mother in a fur coat, a fair-haired boy about seven years old and a nanny dressed in nurse's uniform.

All the sketches in this issue are signed thus, including the Miles Hawk logo modified to hold a bunch of holly in its beak on the back cover, but they are of varying degrees of definition and assurance. The postwar editions of the *"Miles Magazine"* are to have none of such frivolity but are concerned with technical matters and photographic illustrations, some articles in fluent French and the humour confined to an occasional aviation anecdote or the *nom de plume* of the writer such as "Poobare."

Publication of the *"Miles Magazine"* in its original form ceased with the outbreak of war. The resumption in that format recommenced in October 1945; this was a slim edition with a surprising number of advertisements including, interestingly, an advert for *"Kite"* where it seems to stress that this is a quarterly publication with its contributors strictly confined to "aircraft workers" implying aircraft workers of Miles Aircraft. This is an ongoing puzzle as we will see.

The *"Miles Aircraft Works Magazine, War-time Supplement"* was severely curtailed because of the paper shortage, and probably ink, as well as everything else. It was usually confined to a single sheet comprising four pages. It started in May 1942 and by November 23rd 1942 Blossom wrote the title page and leading editorial in a light-hearted way quite out of line with the grim days of the war at that date. She headlines it: "F.G. by ME*"; the "ME" has an asterisk mirrored at the bottom thus: "*M.Miles." Although outwardly jocund, nevertheless there is an undercurrent of vexed impatience and a certain resentment creeps in:

> "F.G. by ME*
>
> I am the editor of this paper and the wife of the Managing Director, F.G. Miles. While you might think that I might be prejudiced on the subject of my husband, I probably know more about him than anyone else here.
>
> Obviously the best way to get to know anybody is to meet them; but as someone pointed out the other day, if F.G. set out

to have a few minutes talk with everyone in the firm, by doing no other work at all, it would take him six weeks (doing full overtime) to complete the task. But nearly everyone at the last discussion wanted more personal contact, so I think it is probably the general wish.

Another thing made me decide to write this article. Once or twice lately I have had remarks made to me which showed that most people haven't the faintest idea what F.G. can do or has done. How should they know? So I thought it would be interesting if I gave a few facts.

Here goes.

F.G. left school at 13 and earned his living in a number of ways. Anything he knows, other than can be taught to a boy of 13, he has taught himself, with the help of friends. In other words he has none of the supposed advantages of an expensive education.

AN ALL ROUNDER

He is a first class pilot, and spent many years teaching, testing and joyriding. He taught himself to design aeroplanes, and can design, stress and build one from beginning to end and then test fly it. He is a good woodworker, a better fitter and an excellent welder. He can use all machine tools and is a practical tool designer and maker. He's done a lot of electrical work and has lately been doing some pretty advanced stuff.

On engines he is sound, though not as brilliant as his brother George at tuning a racing engine. (For those who know what it means F.G. holds 'A,' 'B,' 'C' and 'D' Ground Engineer's Licences and the Instrument Licence.)

He has in fact the knowledge and experience to take on the job of any worker in the factory. I don't say there are not certain jobs that others can do better (I know he can't beat metal as well as someone I know in the Experimental); but I'll bet there are darn few people in this factory or any other who can claim such all round knowledge, experience and skill.

This is a bird's eye view of his workman's skill. Now as head of a large and growing concern, he has other jobs (he would say alas!) to perform. He has had to learn to deal with finance, contracts, mass production, sudden expansion, wartime supplies, labour management, sub-contractors, welfare, advertising, publicity, etc.; and has to have a thorough knowledge of every department in the organisation as well as keeping ahead with current and future design and research. He must be ready to give decisions on any question that is put to him by anybody in the firm, and must be at the beck and call of M.A.P., the Air Ministry, Ministry of Labour, the Ministry of Supply, and the Services. All these things are infinitely more complicated and worrying than merely designing, building and flying an aeroplane – however advanced the design, intricate the work to be done on it, or difficult the machine to fly when finished.

That's a brief outline of what he can do and does. What he is, I realise, can only be found out by personal contact. But I can tell you this as a pointer. He is passionately interested in everything to do with factory life (we talk of little else at home) and would dearly like to be personally acquainted with everyone in the firm and know all that is going on. This is an impossible wish but he does his best. If you've got something you want to tell him, grab him next time you see him pass and spill the beans. (If you don't know what he looks like someone in your shop can probably point him out to you).

HAPPY TOO!

He is very good tempered (although once every ten years or so, at the sight of some injustice, he sees red and has a glorious fight). I disapprove strongly, but I am glad to say that up to the present, thanks to some skill in boxing and a strong fighting spirit, he has always managed to beat his man good and proper.

That's all I can say in the space. (And I hope he doesn't turn me out of house and home for writing like this about him, because – cross my heart – he doesn't know I've done it.) I think he's a grand chap and lots of other people agree with me!"

It sounds as if she was defending him against some sort of adverse criticism. There were bound to be grumbles surfacing under such arduous and depressing circumstances as existed in November 1942, and it appears that she could not bear to think that there was any negative feedback at all against the man who was the love of her life. I find the words "he does his best" especially poignant.

In the same issue there was a report:

> "F.G. Miles was, as he put it, the 'Aunt Sally' at the Discussion Circle Meeting, when twenty-one P. & P. people each told what would be the first three things they would do if they were Managing Director of this Firm."

It may have been this which provoked Blossom to mount the above defence, as she possibly introduced the idea of a Discussion Circle. Certainly we know that she attended, because in the minutes there is a letter from "S. De la Rue (letter read by Mrs Miles)."

In May 1945 Blossom was writing the title page as follows:

> "Dear Readers,
>
> Our third anniversary! How I wish I could have a lovely cake with three candles on it and a slice for all our readers, including the boys still serving in the forces. *[Here she draws a rough sketch of a large birthday cake with some small people lining up with plates in their hands and a man up a ladder lighting a candle.]* Since our last number the longed-for news of the end of the war has come. It won't make a difference to our everyday life for some time to come, but what a lovely relief to our spirits! What seems like aeons ago I imagined myself on VE day doing this *[an arrow pointing to a sketch of her dancing exuberantly with flags in each hand]* while in point of fact this is what I actually did *[here an arrow pointing to her sitting in a deck chair reading a book.]* And I bet most people felt the same way. I know it's the best rest I've had for five years, just because it was a real rest with no feeling of "I ought really to be doing some work."
>
> I hope and believe that by next year's anniversary our men will be pouring back from the East, having finished the Japs as completely as they finished the Nazis.
>
> And I hope that when real peace comes we shall all be together again with more work to do than we know how to cope with!!
>
> My love to you all, home and away.
> Maxine Miles."

This front page was reproduced entirely in her own handwriting, which is small and neat with straight strokes, no loops and no flourishes but not particularly easy to read.

Two years later her style is cosier and very human and warm; the stresses of the war years are gone but there is an undercurrent of unease which she glosses over with a certain glibness. Blossom says in a 1947 edition:

"A few weeks ago J.J. White came to your editor *[herself]* and said that as May 25th was our fifth anniversary he would like a nice piece for the front page. Your editor said that was a splendid idea and she would let him have it in good time. Everybody knows the way days slip by when you have plenty of time to do a job, so here we are with a few days to run and no "nice piece" for the front page.

The editor – (I can't go on in the third person) – I am now faced with the problem of what to say. I thought I could start off as they do in pantomime, with "HERE WE ARE AGAIN" *[here are some sketches of Harlequin and Columbine, some clowns and a dog]* or perhaps more realistically: "HERE WE ARE, STILL GOING STRONG." Never mind. We are still here and after five years' experience feel up to tackling even an earthquake! *[Here she includes sketches of the same characters showing signs of extreme exhaustion, even the dog.]*

Joking apart, it has not been an easy five years for the people who produce this little paper, and I want to thank them on my and your behalf for their successful efforts.

When we started this paper it was published once a fortnight. Then came the *'Wall Newspaper'* which was published more frequently, so about a year ago we decided to make the NEWS a monthly magazine and increase its size to 8 pages. We are glad to say that our sales have kept up so we hope that this means that you still approve of us.

Now comes the hard part of finishing this article. I can think of no fine peroration so I shall end this as I always ended my letters home from school: 'I have no more to say now, so lots and lots of love to all.'

Maxine Miles."

These two little contributions by Blossom say more about her than a dozen learned articles either by her or about her.

In September 1947 we have edition Volume 6 No.8 (still one penny).

"FAREWELL TO THE NEWS

This is the last issue of 'News' to be published for the time being, but certain regular features, notably Exchange & Mart items, will appear in the 'Wall Newspaper.' These and brief accounts of social and sports events, which probably can be accommodated also, should be addressed: Editor, Wall Newspaper, Publicity Dept.

It is a long time since I wrote anything in the 'News' and I have been taken to task about it. I had just made the resolution to write an editorial in each issue, but now the crisis is upon us, so this is in the nature of 'Hail and Farewell.'

As it is necessary to cut down expenditure we have decided to stop printing the 'News' for the time being. The 'Wall Newspaper' will have to take its place.

I have just said that this is 'Hail and Farewell.' It is rather a silly thing to say as the rest of the quotation ('We who are about to die salute thee') is entirely inapt. We are not about to die – far from it, we are about to live. Someone once said that it is easier to die for one's country than to live for her. I think this is certainly true (though one may not believe it at the time) that it is easier to face physical danger than economic danger. For one thing the issue is so much clearer. Physical danger is either there or it is not and absence of body means safety. But economic danger is difficult to assess and absence of body does not avoid this danger.

Britain is going through a bad time at the moment. We are having to do without things which we now call luxuries, but which in more prosperous times would be considered necessities for a happy life. I feel very strongly that we should never lose sight of this. If we do we may find ourselves still doing without when matters improve; we may start to feel that austerity is a good thing in itself, for its own sake. You will know, of course, that I am not pleading for idle luxury, but for the thousand and one little graces of life that make the difference between a hard grind and pleasant living.

It is in this respect that decisions in economy are so difficult. It is so easy to say "we will do without all this or this" when it may prove to be a very false saving. To make a rather exaggerated simile, it is as though one were going to need all one's strength and mind on a fight and so decided to give up eating for fear some of one's energy might be taken up digesting the food. It all boils down, in other words, to finding economic ways of doing things, but not to stop doing them. This I am sure is true – and how easy to say but how difficult to do.

But here is where we all come in. From the largest to the smallest job there is a good way and a bad way of doing it; and the person who does the job is the best one to help work out the good way.

This brings us to another point. How often does one have a good idea only to find that others, whose place it is to cooperate, are not interested. Then comes the moment when one is inclined to give up and say 'I've put up a good idea and nobody will play.' But inertia (the force that makes things and people want to go on the way they are going) has to be coped with. Its course must be altered by applying the brakes or the accelerator, or by turning the wheel. With a machine this is usually effective the first time, but human beings are often a bit pesky and refuse to react to the first pressure. The difficult thing is to apply the pressure without becoming a bore (in which case one is labelled as someone with a bee in his bonnet and who can therefore be disregarded). A tip that we probably all know is to get someone else to give us a hand.

I once put forward a theory that men have been more mechanically inventive than women because they are physically so much lazier. You may imagine the reception I got for this 'outrageous suggestion.' But I still think there is a mite of truth in it. I can still see (with a very imaginative eye, of course) a woman beating up a large dish of eggs and a man coming into the kitchen and saying: 'I could do that in half the time with an electric beater.' I am on the side of this sort of laziness, always provided that the time-saver does the job as well or better than the laborious method. You will notice that my 'laziness' has turned into a pet name for time-saving.

Necessity is also said to be the mother of invention – perhaps necessity is the mother and 'laziness' the father? What a marriage! But it should be a very fruitful one. Necessity is here. Let us all see how much time and effort we can save to meet the situation. Wherever we succeed we shall find that we have achieved economy."

The rather difficult philosophical conclusions Blossom comes to in this strange "peroration," to use her own word, are only explained in the light of events which preceded this editorial. In order to understand this we must go back to the height of the war and the success and glory days of Miles Aircraft under the banner of Phillips & Powis.

CHAPTER 8

COPING WITH THE WAR YEARS

The pressures of war brought with them compensations for firms such as Phillips & Powis. Prewar conditions had meant that nearly all businesses in many fields were struggling financially and so, the situation being common enough, not too much stress went with the constant quest for profitable contracts. By definition, if everyone is in the same boat, no one is much more or any less successful than his neighbour.

The desperate need for vehicles and munitions with which to fight the war, and especially for aircraft which were being destroyed on a daily basis at an horrific rate, led to the government implementing a scheme known as 'cost-plus' for contracts for war necessities. This meant that firms could hardly go wrong; if they made an item, they would always get more for it by a proportion than it cost them to make it. For a lot of companies this was the cliché 'licence to print money' and could lead to exploitation. Miles and Phillips & Powis were never very strong on job-costing and the financial side of the business; it is quite likely that, far from overestimating the cost of producing an aircraft, they may have underestimated it because quite honestly they were thinking of higher things, or things which were to them much more important, like developing more efficient aircraft, better conditions for their workers or inventing technical wonders.

The total turnover for the factory for the whole of the war for Miles was thirty million pounds, and this was more than they had ever thought of even in their dreams, but nobody had a clear idea of how this was made up. F.G. bought the Rolls Royce holding of company shares in 1941. These had just been converted from Preference Shares into Ordinary Shares and might have amounted to some sixty thousand pounds, probably equivalent to six million at today's values. Certainly no one envisaged the excess profit tax which the government was to impose after the war in the drive to recoup some of the debts the nation had incurred in fighting the war, and which meant a long period of austerity and 'tightening one's belt' for the people of Britain. This tax was to be imposed at the astonishing rate of one hundred per cent.

In the early part of the war a significant personal event took place for Blossom. Her Aunt Maxine died in France. She lived in her villa Le Château de l'Horizon on the French Riviera. This villa was made famous by the very competent and artistic semi-impressionist painting that Winston Churchill had executed on one of his many visits there, which is often exhibited and reproduced. Unfortunately Maxine did not live long enough to see him become Prime Minister.

She had had several breakdowns in her health, mainly because of her over-indulgence in food, wine and life itself. She had become incredibly fat, and her obesity resulted in symptoms for which she refused to take measures like cutting down sugar and salt but continued her lifestyle until she had a stroke. Miraculously she recovered from this stroke without any paralysis and went on gaily as before. There was consternation from her family when the war started. France was too near Germany to be considered safe, even though the capitulation of France was not thought likely initially. The Mediterranean coastline was obviously a strategic target anyway and all her family and friends urged Maxine to leave; she could easily have gone to the United States where she had investments already. However she was ultra-conservative and called F.D. Roosevelt "the madman in the White House," and of course there had been passenger ships sunk in the Atlantic in the first few days of the conflict. It may have simply been that she was too fond of her magnificent home with its equally magnificent views to leave it; at any rate, she refused to contemplate leaving France.

Her many friends rallied round. Noël Coward made a great effort to overcome all the bureaucracy and travelled over to see her before the war shut down all forms of unneccessary foreign travel; he urged her to come back with him. A lot of her guests were young men and they were called up into the forces, so they had to leave and gradually she was left with none of her glittering social life. She complained that few wrote to her, she said that Winston Churchill was the one who wrote most often and that was because, she thought, he had more time than anyone else!

Eventually her health gave way in a serious fashion, and from being enormously obese she became painfully thin; this enhanced her enormous eyes which had always held such an hypnotic effect on her admirers, and her hair had turned completely white. Nevertheless she still managed to play a big part in the war effort. She organised all the local women into knitting parties to knit 'comforts' for the troops, she gave parties to all the children of the area and gave large sums of money to the poor, many of whom were destitute because their husbands and fathers were in prison. It was largely a Communist area and so there were a lot of internees; in Valauris, as elsewhere, Communists were considered a security risk. Maxine did not allow her political sympathies to stop her aiding the families of the extreme left-wing supporters. She even provided footballs for them.

Finally she died on March 5th 1940. Blossom and F.G. had to get special Home Office permission to go out to the funeral. This was extremely difficult, especially as they had to fly within the time scale that was obviously vital. It is doubtful that any ordinary mortals could have succeeded in getting the necessary dispensation, but Blossom could pull a few strings, both on the flying side and among the Establishment. It was a flying visit in more ways than one, and one fraught with danger. Even Winston Churchill did not risk going to the funeral of his very special old friend, but he sent a telegram to George Keppel who was still, against all odds and all advice, staying out at Le Château de l'Horizon and asked him to be his representative at Maxine's funeral.

The Last Post was played over her grave by her Chasseurs and they fired a volley in spite of the war situation. She was buried in the Protestant Cemetery at Cannes. Later Blossom was asked to take her Aunt's place at a ceremonial in which the Poste Château de l'Horizon was presented with the fanion that Maxine had just had made for them. Posthumously she became the marraine of the regiment . . .

Blossom and F.G. had to hurry through the ceremony and formalities, order a headstone for her grave and then try to sort through her aunt's desk and effects. In the exigencies of the time all they could do was bring back a few papers of a legal nature and Maxine's jewellery.

Gertrude was living in Kent, in St. Margaret's Bay, Sir Johnston having died three years before. Blossom went to her mother to tell her of the funeral and what they had been able to do. She told her that she had ordered a headstone in accordance with what she imagined her mother would have wanted.

"It's a plain granite headstone with a simple inscription that just says 'Maxine Elliot' and the dates, 'Born 1873, died 1940.'"

Gertrude, who had never got over her nervous habit of clicking her fingernails against her teeth, said: "Oh! dear, oh! dear."

"Well, isn't that right?" Blossom asked.

Gertrude nervously replied: "It's just that naughty little Dettie was never quite truthful about her age. It ought to be 1869."

The ironic fact was that even Gertrude, her own sister, had it wrong by a year, she had actually been born in 1868. Even so she was only seventy-one by March 1940.

She left an estate of over a million dollars to be divided amongst her family, equivalent to a hundred million today.

*   *   *

Meanwhile, back at Woodley, the pace of life was hotting up. The previous chapter which mentioned the *"Miles Magazine"* showed how exhausted Blossom and everyone else was by the time Victory in Europe Day came, but while the war went on no one had time to consider if they were tired or not. Blossom had more or less open house for all and sundry. As Lands End House was so near to the airfield it was inevitable that all sorts of people and personnel should gravitate towards it. Perfect strangers were invited by Blossom to have hot baths, warm drinks and food, remembered gratefully to this day by some of the recipients of her hospitality in the days of shortages of every type of food and fuel.

Mr P.A. Bentley was a young conscript whose unit was diverted after various crises to Woodley aerodrome and was detailed to clear wooded areas, dig slit trenches and build block houses to mount Lewis guns and guard the airfield and entrances to the factory and hangars.

He says: "The Directors F. and G. Miles and Blossom welcomed us and we were occasionally invited to their home for food, drink and baths."

This was in April and May 1940 and these young lads were muddy, cold, tired, hungry and far from home. Mr Bentley remembers Tommy Rose in a Master chasing a German bomber "armed only with a revolver"! Amy Johnson was most approachable when she was delivering aircraft for the Air Transport Auxiliary and took time to talk to the lowly squaddies. A great fuss was evidently under way one day with blanco, spraying tin helmets in the paint shop and glueing ill-fitting forage caps on undersized heads with aero-adhesive in the belief that Winston Churchill was about to pay a visit, but in the end he went to Langley airfield instead. Magisters were rolling off the production line, Spitfires were being overhauled and serviced, and there were often accidents on the airfield, some minor due to heavy landings, some major.

These reminiscences illustrate the frenzied activity that was taking place all over the country but especially at such sites as Woodley. In the factory Blossom and F.G. were taking part in all sorts of activities which showed how committed they were to the morale of their workforce. Although when one young girl, now Mrs Barker, was sent from the print shop up to F.G.'s office (Blossom's office was just opposite), she was literally trembling with nerves at having to speak to the great man, there are photographs which prove how informal Blossom and F.G. could be. There is a photograph of Blossom with her arm rather drunkenly draped around the neck of a man much shorter than her and another where she and F.G. are hardly recognisable at a "Tarts and Tramps" party, Blossom dressed as a scruffy man, eyes closed, fag in mouth, and F.G. as an ugly old woman in a headscarf.

In many ways, the events which were to overtake Blossom and F.G. after the war were as much a product of mental and physical exhaustion as they were due to economic factors. Even so it was to be more than galling to think that after all this supreme effort on their parts they were not to be rewarded for it . . . quite the reverse.

In spite of all the activity of waging war, something happened in 1942 that was to change some people's lives for ever.

Blossom was the prime mover in a scheme that had an incalculable influence on the lives of at least three hundred people and, by osmosis, on their children and probably grandchildren too. Her application and dedication to the scheme had also a far-reaching effect on worldwide aviation, even on everyone who flies in an airliner today.

It happened like this: Blossom's penchant for 'collecting people' led to the Miles's becoming acquainted with a refugee from Hungary, Dr Tibor Csato (pronounced "Charter"). He was introduced to them by Helen Kirkpatrick who was an American, a journalist and one of Blossom's circle of friends.

Dr Csato had advanced theories on education, especially scientific education, which he had expounded at great lengths to Helen Kirkpatrick. With Americans usually being more prepared to take eccentric ideas seriously than the staid British established dons, she saw that Blossom's unique qualities would be likely to be sympathetic to Csato's tenets and so the meeting was set up.

Csato had written a paper on his theory (or theories, because there were several, seven in fact), but the main idea was that: "People can learn faster than people can teach." The other ideas were perhaps not so startling, as they have surreptitiously been absorbed into modern-day teaching without really being recognised as such. They are mainly about the setting of goals, the value of combining experience with study and the marriage of practical work with theoretical study.

In 1993 at the age of ninety, Dr Csato was to write from Munich:

"How quickly 50 years fly past! It seems only yesterday that I first visited F.G. Miles and put to him the scheme of M.A.T.S. [Miles Aircraft Technical School] and he endorsing it fullheartedly. "It is what I've been searching for but in the dark all of my life" were his unforgettable words. And now 50 years have flown by and our old students and teachers from all parts of the world and all the diverse walks of life are coming to Berkshire with a long sustained sense of togetherness.

It is truly wonderful to know that the spirit behind our venture is still alive – largely due to my friend Walter Evans.

Alas it is not possible for me to make September 11th but I
send you all my wishes for the present and the future and wish
you a joyous reunion.

Tibor Csato."

Once the idea of an aeronautical technical school run on the lines of
Dr Csato's theories were in F.G.'s mind, he handed over the actual
operation of it to be overseen by Blossom; she was more than
enthusiastic and added a great many of her own ideas too.

To put ideas into action needed two main elements: teachers
and students. The latter might have been more difficult to obtain
than the former. The meeting with Tibor Csato took place in the
autumn of 1942; by the spring of 1943 the school was well
advanced. The initial nucleus of pupils was obtained by taking the
cream of the apprentices from the factory and some of "Blossom's
Babies" from the trainee draughtswomen of Liverpool Road. In
fact, at first the students were actually paid a wage for going to
school – *there* was initiative and incentive in action!

To find teachers with similar ideas to Tibor Csato was easier
than one might suppose. There had been *avant garde* proposals
circulating in the fringes of education in the twenties and thirties;
the Peckham Experiment was a famous example. Some of these
were fed by left-wing political ideas, pacifism and vegetarianism,
and some by the more bizarre theories of naturism, free love and
free association of ideas.

One thing that would strike the observer today was that all the
teachers of theory were very young, only the practical teachers were
more mature. William Walter Evans was chosen to be headmaster.
His background was a strange mixture of subjects. He was an
ordained priest but had also been a nuclear scientist working on the
Manhattan Project. This duality was to come to the fore when the
atomic bombs were first tested; he was sure that there would be a
chain reaction and the world would come to an end, so pupils at the
school hostel were rather startled to find him dressed in his clerical
robes as a preparation for this. He was born on June 2nd 1915, and
therefore was only in his twenty-eighth year when the school
started, and he had already had a very full experience of life, having
had a peripatetic childhood and what may have been a nervous

breakdown as well, as a result of his conscience about working on nuclear fission.

He interviewed the other tutors who were to teach structures, aerodyamics and the related subjects necessary to design and build aircraft. One of them, Alan Pepper, made an immediate impression when he referred to the Peckham Experiment and was given the job on the spot. He and David Marples were especially gifted not only in their subjects but in putting their ideas across to the students and inspiring them in the thirst for knowledge. Other tutors, not so academically qualified, nevertheless possessed a genius for bringing light to any theory or practical notion that had previously merely been an academic jigsaw puzzle to conventionally-taught pupils. A strange weld of academics, practically gifted teachers and the students themselves – who were expected to do some of the teaching – took place in an atmosphere of almost mystical completeness.

Blossom took a very active interest in the school. She instigated sports activities, and every Wednesday afternoon was given over to rowing on the nearby river at Sonning or similar physical events. She organised annual athletic meetings at the sports stadium in Palmer Park; she always came to these bringing her small daughter Mary – Jeremy by that time was at Harrow. She gave lectures to the students on, sometimes, entirely unrelated subjects; she gave them facilities for film shows, usually artistic, impenetrable foreign films. She arranged for an amateur dramatic society to be set up among the students and paid for the services of a coach, Mark Everard, who had been active in the Phillips & Powis Players. She regularly visited the school and took part in a Pathé News Film about the school which was shown in cinemas all over the country.

She also gave lectures around the country on the school, on Miles Aircraft and related subjects, often to Aeromodelling Clubs, and from at least one of these, in Brighton, two more young men were inspired with the idea of the Technical School and approached Blossom afterwards, asking if there was any chance of becoming students there. In no time at all they were taking their place at the Woodley college.

The time and money which this cost was given generously and willingly because she shared the ideal that a complete education, not only in aeronautical engineering but in the finer points of art appreciation and of life itself, was an ultimate goal that was not only desirable but achievable.

Some of her lectures are vividly remembered by the students. One lecture she gave was on French mediaeval costume with illustrations drawn by herself, large sheets of paper hung over a blackboard and turned over in series. It might seem a peculiar subject for a lecture to engineering students, but another similar lecture made even more of an impression on some of the boys when she was graphically illustrating how the fashion for 'enhancing' the codpieces of the young man-about-town of that period was attained.

Her wide social circle was echoed in those she somehow persuaded to come and lecture to her students; they included personalities and academics. Guy Gibson V.C. (who led the famous 'Dambuster' raid), Major Lewis Hastings, Monsignor Vance and Ludovic Kennedy were among the lecturers to the main school. The music group had lectures from Alan Pepper on 'the sonata form,' the film group meetings were opened by the music of the "Waltz of the Flowers" and was presided over by Lewis Budd. F.G. gave talks on advanced film projectors.

At the end of the session of study, which was intended to be a four-year course, but in fact, had to be curtailed for the later intake of students because of the economic collapse of the firm, there was a choice of professional degree examination. Most opted for the Associate Fellowship of the Royal Aeronautical Society, naturally, while others took the professional qualifications of the Institute of Mechanical Engineers. Whatever qualification they sought, the idea was that the training (with practical work in the mornings in the woodshop, fitting shop, machine shop, engines hangar, drawing office, stress office, aerodynamics department and with lectures in the afternoons) meant that by the end of their course they were qualified to design an aircraft and build it themselves from scratch – and many did!

At the beginning of the school, some pupils even constructed some of the buildings and not long after that they made their own wind-tunnel. The pupils did actually design and build a twin-engined high-wing monoplane and called it the "Venture." This was almost complete when the school had to be taken over by Reading Technical College so that the students could complete their degrees after Miles Aircraft no longer existed at Woodley. The aircraft had to be destroyed: this was historically very disappointing, but future archivists were not the main preoccupation at the time. Other projects had been in the pipeline, an ultralight aircraft being one of them.

Strange to say, while the school was still in its early stages, Blossom also set up an agricultural technical school. Some of the pupils opted to transfer to this and they remember taking the milk in churns to Lands End House early in the mornings. One wonders if this was more a pragmatic exercise than an idealistic one in the light of extreme food shortages and rationing, but at least one of these students took to farming as a career and has remained in it to this day.

The criteria by which students were accepted into the school were eclectic to the 'n'th degree. This led to an extraordinary mix and blend of cultures, nationalities and varying academic abilities. There were pupils who had close relationships to the royal family, sons of famous sculptresses and artists, sons and daughters of political and aristocratic connections, children of army families, children of film stars, refugees, displaced persons, Czechs, Israelis, Indians and Anglo-Indians, Turks, French and more, all learning and working in total unremarked unison with those from local schools and trades. There were those with brilliant original minds and those who were thoroughly 'run-of-the-mill.'

There were residential hostels for most of the pupils who did not live within day-school range. These varied with the intake of students. Sandford Manor, conveniently situated on the perimeter track of the airfield, was at one time a co-educational hostel and later was just for girls only. Walter Evans and his wife Helen also lived at Sandford Manor for part of the time as live-in 'housemaster and matron.' For a time the girls lived in the Manor House while the boys resided in Nissen huts in the garden where conditions were primitive to the extreme. The boys themselves had to take it in turns to empty the portable chemical lavatories, not a task they liked, and it was also very cold most of the time. They kept up a good supply of home-made cider and other nefarious activities and there was a certain amount of 'free love' going on between grounds and house; perhaps it was this that led to the boys eventually being housed in another hostel at Sindlesham Mill about three miles away!

The proportion of boys to girls in the school was of course rather overwhelming but the girls proved to be just as successful academically and went on to work in the aircraft industry, even being involved in such projects as the design and stressing of Concorde. There was no doubt that Blossom was a role model for them. As Blossom said in one of her articles, she started off with thirty boys and thirty girls but by 1947 there were only eight girls and by the time the school came to an end in 1949 there were only two girls.

A very large percentage of the boys attained high positions not only in the aviation industry but in a wide variety of professions including the oil industry, journalism and film directing, but what is most remarkable is the fact that many of the very top positions in companies like British Aerospace and Boeing were occupied by those who had formerly been pupils at the Miles Aeronautical Technical School. Would Boeing have achieved its premier status in world aviation without the input of Miles Aeronautical Technical School?

The difference between M.A.T.S. and other technical colleges was subtle and yet glaring at the same time. This was not only because of the main precepts but because every aspect was explored, sometimes from sheer necessity but more often out of informed choice. The main subjects concerned with constructing an aircraft and passing examinations were superimposed on manufacturing one's own machine tools, jigs and test equipment. New ways of performing experiments and testing theories were combined with making the actual apparatus needed. Councils and committees to run the school like a factory, and tutorials and convocations to run it like a university, were entirely democratic with pupils and teachers taking equal parts.

All these ideals were put into motion against the most difficult conditions of one of the most stressful periods in British history. Several of the winters of the war years and immediately postwar were among the most severe of the century. Sometimes the airfield was covered in snow, sometimes in dense fog, sometimes waterlogged. Most schools had to be closed for lack of fuel, and the 'British Restaurant' scheme for serving school dinners meant that the food served at M.A.T.S. was at times hardly edible. If there had not been a village baker within cycling range who still somehow managed to fill his doughnuts with jam several students might have been seriously malnourished. At least one of them, Gunter Bierman, claimed to have lived on bread alone in order to save his money for more important things like taking his girl friend out. The depth and complexity of some of the philosophic discussions that manifested themselves during the lunch breaks were balanced by the typical student-type pranks like putting sand in the tank of the headmaster's putty-coloured Standard Nine.

Ingenuity in finding any sort of fuel for the black 'Tortoise' stoves which inadequately heated a small corner of the hangars led to some rather dangerous practices, some done with the best of experimental intentions! This also applied to searching for fuel for a few motorbikes. Thus a throughly mind-stretching 'all-round' education was obtained.

After the war was over – and we have already read Blossom's thoughts on her immediate reaction to that in the editorial of the little magazine – the possiblities of publishing more advanced periodicals and journals came with the easing of restrictions on newsprint. In 1946 an elegant volume called *"Milestones"* was published and sold for ten shillings and sixpence which was about a tenth of the average weekly salary at the time. There were also small format booklets called "Milestones" which were written by Don Brown and contained facts and figures and illustrations about the aircraft the firm had produced. These have no relevance to the larger book which is a very significant publication and reveals a great deal about Blossom.

The large format *"Milestones"* contained articles and drawings by some very prestigious figures. Felix Topolski contributed some drawings of Miles Master production lines, the machine shop, the press shop, even "Tea Up!" on the assembly lines. These were repoduced on art paper and were meant to be framed if desired. The Earl of Portsmouth, Hugh Bergel and Joanna Tomlin were just a few of the other notable names. An anthology of poetry was included along with erudite technical and political articles. The photographs by Robert Capa, another of Blossom's family friends, are stunning.

The choice of the poems, including "Love's Secret" by William Blake juxtaposed by "The Old Stoic" by Emily Brontë, poems of the fourteenth, fifteenth and sixteenth century, and those of Robert Herrick and Christina Rossetti, all beautifully set out and headed by James Elroy Flecker's "If There Ever Shall Arise a Nation" speaks loudly of Blossom's personal philosophy. A long article by her called "To Live and Learn" shows this directly so here it is quoted in full. Some of the text is a direct quotation from Dr Csato but she thoroughly agreed with its sentiments; and a great deal of her own words may not be too interesting to the modern reader, but as it is not possible to decide which parts she would have considered most important, to précis it would be unfair. The full text is as follows:

"TO LIVE AND LEARN
by Maxine Miles

This is the story of an experiment in education. It is not the sort of experiment which begins 'I wonder what would happen if we did thus and thus.' We know very well what would happen if we can find a way to carry out our ideas. The experimental part is *how* to find the way.

About four years ago Dr Csato was introduced to us as a man who had written an extremely interesting paper on the broad principles of technical education, and was anxious to get advice and criticism from an industrialist on certain aspects of it. My husband read the paper, found that it expressed clearly ideas and ideals about which we had been vaguely talking and thinking for some time, and immediately decided that advice and criticism were useless without experience and that therefore the only thing to do was to start at once and try and put those ideas into practice.

These ideas and ideals are centred round our belief that man has a right to be happy, that happiness is only attainable if the whole man is healthy and that therefore no system of living can achieve this unless a full chance is given to each human being to develop his body, his mind and his spirit. These three attributes cannot be separated; it is useless to create a society

137

in which the members are as well cared for as a herd of prize cattle if they have nothing on which to feed their minds and spirits. A world where man's body is cared for and his mind given food will still be uneasy and lost if the spirit is earthbound. And, while a community whose minds and spirits are free may have a better chance of a happy life, that life, without bodily health, will not be a very long one!

We therefore believe that every man has the right, and society the duty, to develop each to the full of his capabilities. Dr Csato reached these conclusions by seeing what a miserable, worried, sickly creature modern man has become in spite of all his boasted technical advance. My husband came to the same conclusion, by seeing what a mess this same man made of his technical advances in spite of his boasted better living conditions.

What are the standards of value which determine the conventional layout of our technical education? This we can best see by analysing our accepted system.

The aim of present day technical education is to acquire technical skill by the shortest possible route. There must be no other subjects, nor must there be any wasteful broadening of the technical curriculum itself. To acquire knowledge means to pass an examination, to graduate, to qualify for a job. This is, of course, the sole aim of this type of education. The plan and the action being adjusted to the aim, the curriculum is cut to fit a given job. The textbook from which we can learn by heart all the answers to the questions likely to be asked at the examination is considered the ideal textbook.

Unfortunately, it so happens that technique does not stay put. By this time the training, so uncompromisingly useful, is completed, technique has changed and the job, too, has either changed or become out of date.

The students entering the technical school can know little more but that the job for which they want to be trained is safe, and that the prospects are good and that the curriculum is reputed to make them fit to take it in the shortest possible time. Once there, no matter what their natural capacities, all are hurried along the same narrow groove from school to job. Indeed they would resent it if they were not.

When they arrive into the safety of their haven, the job, they start to make or do something, one little bit of a big complicated job: the commodity which was in demand when they first began to learn. Time saving and utility in the strict and narrow sense of the word is again the slogan. They cannot change or try other things, or go about to understand the wholeness of production, nor can they study the present and guess the future demands of society. There is little time and they were brought up not to look beyond their benches. It would be unforgivable – and indeed in terms of the existing organisation dangerous – to interrupt repetitive skill and smooth production (no matter whether there is a demand for the product or not). The aim is to produce more and more of a given commodity, faster and ever faster, with less and less expenditure of skill and intelligence.

As soon as organisation is perfected and production fully rationalised, with everyone trained to fill his niche, the demands have changed and new technical developments have – maybe against the same heavy odds – arisen somewhere else.

It is interest and necessity for worker and employer alike to continue the production of the same commodity in growing quantities. This is not wicked, it is natural. People have to live, to keep their families, to keep their livelihood and they are trapped in the narrow grooves of a system of production and, together with it, a mode of thinking. The individual shares no interest, no responsibility, even with the next door department, not to mention the community in the wider sense. The job was useful. To maintain it was right. What threatens its continuity is wrong. Soon the uncompromising usefulness of the technical training of rationalised production with its extreme division of labour and responsibility results in the fight for the sectional interests of the day before yesterday.

The worker, bored by mind-killing monotony, tired and worried about the future, is antagonistic and irritated, and blames obvious and superficial symptoms instead of trying to find out what is fundamentally wrong.

Labour relations are strained. The producers of not-needed commodities fight to restrict the making of those which are needed, they fight against import of goods which are cheaper and better, agitate against countries which produce them or those which buy them in preference to theirs. One trade is set against the other, one section of the population is the enemy of the other, classes blame each other for their plight. There is no pause, no release from the complex and destructive clash of interests; no stopping to consider the final aim of life, the standards set for its attainment and a reconsideration of the present plans and actions in their light. This is impossible, for there are no other standards but the material security of today. Youth, in a world adrift and distraught, grows up in fear of unemployment and apprehension of wars to come. It reaches out for safety for immediate security and the circle starts again . . .

Our solution to this problem as far as technical education is concerned is that boys and girls should have the widest possible technical education, during the course of which they may not only learn as many as possible of the techniques that go to make their particular trade, but during this period they may find out in which branch their talents and preferences lie. In order to do this in reality the work they do must be real and purposeful. From the first day of their training they must start on real work so that they learn as they make. In the same way the theoretical work must be as real as possible and always closely allied to the practical work in hand. (Many people will remember the difficulties of the abstract problem in school mathematics and some will recognise their different approach to these problems when they had to be solved for some practical purpose!) But this idea only covers the skill, craftsmanship and technique of any particular work. More important still is the habit of working in a team.

I quote Dr Csato again. He wrote in his original thesis on Technical Training:

'The unit of the Centre is the independent responsible group. Its size will fluctuate, according to the work it is engaged on, between 8 and 24.

The following are held to be essential pre-conditions in order that organised group-work may develop into inspired team-work:

1. The task assigned to each group must be of a nature to give those engaged in it a sense of common purpose.

2. Responsibility must be individual, but the measure of merit is common achievement.

3. The purpose must have recognised and understood value to society, present and future.

4. In order to heighten its consciousness of purpose, each group must bear some practical responsiblity for both the immediate and long-range consequences of its activities.

5. Each member must be used (with the necessary latitude for quick functional adjustment) to the full extent of his capacities. The effectiveness of this principle is ensured by:

(a) the empirically proved axiom of *natural selection*. It is in the interest of all that each should be used to the best of his natural faculties.

(b) by maintaining the principle of apprenticeship throughout the training. Each member (and every instructor) will be teacher and apprentice at the same time, not only through each becoming a member of several teams, but also within one and the same team. By giving a hand to the newly arrived apprentice, by working out new methods of processing, cooperation etc. – in these and other ways each member can remain fresh and adaptable while becoming highly skilled in his main task.

(c) by many-sided training. Training must be simultaneous not only in the main tasks and duties of the Centre, but also in the various details (even on entirely different levels) of one and the same task.

This is what is meant by many-sided training in skill, initiative and purpose. It is education in the technique and spirit of teamwork. In the last analysis, it is ethical education in the most inspiring sense, making both learning and leisure creative, bringing about self-fulfillment through self-discipline and identifying ambition with "the good life."'

These are our ideas and we are convinced that if we can put them into practice we shall get the results. But, as I said in the beginning, the experiment lies in how to do it.

We opened our school in March 1943 with about 30 girls and 30 boys. As it was in the middle of the war we were unable to build, and so made use of two large farm barns, some small outbuildings, wooden huts, and two Robin dispersal hangars. We collected equipment and machinery as we went along and now, after more than three years, we have a fine machine shop and a well-equipped drawing office and laboratory. The school has designed and made its own wind tunnel, smoke tunnel and sound projector for showing films. The library has been a difficulty as there has been such a woeful shortage of books whether technical or otherwise; however we are gradually collecting a good stock. During this period the students designed and did the working drawings for converting a cornstore into an excellent canteen and lavatory block.

So much for the physical aspect of the school.

We started with a small teaching staff who were not trained instructors but just enthusiasts from drawing offices, machine shop, fitting shop and wood shop. We have since been joined by others, and our staff now consists of a headmaster and nine assistants who are responsible for aerodynamics, stress, design, laboratory, production and engines, drawing, woodwork, fitting and machine work. We also have two part-time physical training instructors. All instructors will agree that, while holding firmly to the principles of our beliefs, the difficulty is to put such beliefs into practice. It is one thing to say that training must be purposeful and quite another to invent ways of making it so. It is even more difficult to ensure that the theoretical training shall be vitally tied up with the practical work that is going on, for while it is essential to have a good background of theoretical principles it is our contention that such principles must never be studied in a vacuum and that the surest way to understanding of a theory is the opportunity to put that theory into immediate practice.

Here is the kernel of our experiment, and this is where the pattern of the school is constantly changing. We have made our mistakes and had our successes. The experiment is still going on and it is too early as yet to draw any conclusions or to lay down any hard and fast dicta as to how our methods should be applied. At the time of writing this is how the school runs.

We take in boys or girls of sixteen years old, either from the factory or from outside. We ask for no particular educational qualifications, but make our selection by interview to judge the type of intelligence and to make sure that the prospective student is keen to come.

The course runs from three to four years. The first year with us is really a selection period and at the end of that time we and the student should be able to decide what is their bent and their preference.

The year is divided into three fifteen-week terms and during the first year all the students get a practical basic training in woodwork, fitting, machine work, drawing, elementary design, elementary engineering and laboratory work. They have lectures in mathematics, physics, mechanics, work-shop practice, theory of machines, etc.

At the end of the first year some will have to continue their training as craftsmen either in our factory or elsewhere and some will stay for a second year at the school to continue drawing, stress, aerodynamics etc. These become members of one of the teams which are designing and making some type of aeroplane in the school. (The present teams, for instance, are designing and building a 5,000 lb twin-engined aeroplane which should be flying before Christmas.) At the end of the second year some students will go out as junior draughtsmen, while others – those whom we may expect to become the future executives – will stay for a third year studying to be designers or production engineers. At the end of the three-year course students should be able to sit for the A.F.R.Ae.S. or the A.M.I.Mech.E.

Besides the daily lectures there is a tutorial system. Certain instructors have a number of second or third year students under their care; they see these boys and girls once a week, helping them with any difficulties and making sure their studies are well balanced. As the instructors have a wide range of interests outside their technical knowledge, the tutorials are likely to range over a very broad field and so help to make certain that the earnest student does not confine his interests to cramming technical subjects. It is no uncommon thing to find a tutor and student deep in a discussion on biology or on how to study classical music.

This is the broad structure of the training curriculum at present, but there are many other activities outside the technical training which form a living part of the school.

One afternoon a week is given up to games and outside lectures and cinema shows. The outside lecture may be on any subject and is given by someone who is at the top of their profession or who has specialised knowledge. It may be on art, ethics, science, political trends, history or adventure! The following day two hours are spent in discussion groups (never more than ten to a group) when any subject the group chooses is discussed. The groups may choose their own leaders who are given a short course by our headmaster in the art of discussion leading.

There is a school committee, elected each term, on which are represented members of the school and staff, which sits once a week and acts as an advisory body to the headmaster. This committee is responsible for many of the outside activities of the school, such as sports, entertainments and canteen.

We have not had enough time yet to draw any but the broadest conclusions from our experiment. One thing is certain, however, and that is that if you give young people a chance to do advanced work and do not make it sound difficult they will be doing skilled jobs, both manual and mental, in a few months. Most people have suffered in their lives from having been told that some trade or profession is very hard and will take years of practice to master. While it is true that nothing can replace experience it is also true that the quicker and earlier you are allowed to try the sooner you will gain the experience. There is one small crab in this that has to be overcome. If a student is given a hard task and does it reasonably easily, he is inclined to think that it is not true, that he has somehow taken a short cut, that there is a trick in it somewhere. Our students have designed, stressed and built a twin-engined aeroplane and still regard it with a slight measure of disbelief. In the same way those who have gone to the factory have discovered that the work is simpler than they anticipated and cannot help wondering if they have not been lucky in falling into such an easy job. We feel that this is a difficulty that is well worth overcoming if not ignoring!

I should like to end this article with another quotation from Dr Csato's address to the school as I think it sums up our aims, which we have only faintly begun to see a way of achieving but which we hope and believe we shall attain one day.

'Education must, in our opinion, be concerned with much more than making people technically fitted for a job. It should be concerned with developing mind, body and character. It should query and answer the questions of how people should live and what they should be. Of all these, technical education is but one part, though an essential part. Education should encourage the student to query the object of life instead of taking for granted that it is nothing but one's livelihood.

But this is not all: it is my conviction that the sanity of the individual, the harmony of society, the survival and the progress of the nation may be secured only when the conduct of life comes from three main springs, and that it is from them that the standards of education must be derived. These three springs are faith, the vision of a better tomorrow, the discipline of today.

It must be the three together, not one or the other or two without the third.

By faith, I mean broadly, the common tenets which we have held in Europe for several thousand years, the belief in God: in the Universe, created by Him; in Man, made in His image, imperfect but endowed by free will to choose and perfect or deface the image of God . . .

Inseparable from this Faith are: the distress over one's present imperfection; the wish and the continued effort to change.

145

Out of the Faith and the deep dissatisfaction with oneself and with the world as they are now, rises the visionary image of a different, a better state of mankind in the future: the vision of tomorrow.

Those who strive in a common plan to realise this vision are bound to share the continued effort, the duties and the rules, essential to the progress towards attainment; the discipline of the present.

To work together now on a common plan in order to realise the vision of a better future demands of each of us to give our best and to become our best. It demands the full development and best use of human beings: acknowledges, encourages and insists on the enjoyment of the natural differences between them.

This width of vision and the right perspective of things to be feared and of things not to be feared make for daring and enterprise. The whole of life and of history teaches that one can gain only by abnegation. With all the obligations, duties and the call on continued effort, goes yet a carefree serenity concerning the petty attachments and worries of the present. Work and pleasure, service and joy, self-interests and duties towards our fellow human beings merge into it.

You can see for yourself how these standards of life want education to view the object of life in the first, the object of livelihood in the second place and that they demand education of the entire person: the detection and development to the full of his inborn capacities of mind, body and character.

Modern life is stultified by the lack of that vision which raised even the humdrum into the realm of the creative; that vision of three-fold harmony which is the vision of the Good.

I do not think it matters too much what I and my generation, or those older than we, think or say: the decision and the future lie with you, the young people of England.'"

Blossom concludes with her own words:

"It is true that the future lies with the young people of any generation in any age, but their actions in years to come may well be barren or fruitful according to the nourishment these children receive while they are young and growing. It is therefore the task of this generation to make sure that the next shall be offered the best it is in our power to give. Our school is our way of attempting this duty."

What is most remarkable, apart from its content, in the last extract is the radical change of Blossom's literary style from previously published articles. The whimsical, quirky style of the editorials in the *"Works Magazine"* has been replaced by a severely disciplined language and construction. This discipline was to be a characteristic of her later years as remembered by her son and by some of her students.

Something else which is, too, most remarkable is the extreme contrast between both the form and content of Blossom's "To Live and Learn" and the contribution by F.G. in this same magazine called "Justice or Tyranny."

Although she is cautious in attributing too much success to her 'experiment in education' without more years of experience to test it, nevertheless the tone and conclusions of her writing have an optimistic, serene air full of hope and confidence in the future and of mankind.

In contrast F.G. writes with deep bitterness and resentment. He starts off by saying that the state has taken the place of God and then goes on to claim that:

"Tyranny is after all only a frightful kind of Freedom: perhaps not even a different kind," *(and continues:)* ". . . when Justice is thrown out for the right of a Home Secretary, a monopoly, or, for that matter, a Trade Union Leader . . . we recognise with inescapable clarity (those of us not blinded by propaganda nor deafened by slogans) that freedom is lost and justice, which is the only good basis of human community, thrown aside like a discarded drab."

(He continues:) "Let us not deceive ourselves. Gradually year by year a new attitude towards justice and freedom is growing in these islands. The old clear issues of right and wrong are being clouded over."

(He uses such phrases as) "bureaucratic anonymity and immunity from responsiblity, petty tyrants," *and claims of* "farmers driven to suicide and their widows robbed of possession by Government representatives."

He says that *internal [his italics]* letters are censored, and are being steamed open and resealed by government departments and that there are other abuses of privacy and people's rights.

> *(Also:)* "We have had inspectors sent to determine whether a newly married couple should have a single bed or a double."
> *(He warns that:)* "Tyranny is always better organised than Freedom."

How these two could have lived together in harmony with these opposing philosophies is difficult to imagine, but maybe it is sometimes with people as it always is with magnetism: opposites attract. The articles illustrate more of the differences of their early lives and how they were each affected by their childhood than how more than a decade of marriage to each other could modify these approaches.

By 1946 F.G. was beginning to see what looked like a betrayal of his ideals and his dedication to the future of the British aircraft industry. He had wholeheartedly believed that all his wartime efforts would be rewarded by postwar recognition, both in status and financial terms. Disillusionment was setting in; far from being the utopia most people imagined would accompany the end of a long and arduous struggle, the postwar period was attended by worse deprivation and problems than most of the war had been, and without the stimulus of the ideals of patriotism to inspire.

In the same magazine F.G. also wrote an article of a more technical nature called "Feeder Line"; this is a projection of how he envisaged future passenger air traffic would progress. He had proved to be right in all his forecasts such as "the minimum economic size of airline aeroplanes will grow larger" and "the number and complexity of flying aids necessary to safety will increase," and "no matter how high or fast or far the giant transport craft may fly, their paths will be shaped according to the world's centres of population." But unfortunately his plans and dreams for the Miles Marathon and the Merchantman in this scenario were not to be realised commercially; although there are many aircraft looking incredibly like the Merchantman proving invaluable in their particular niches today.

Another publication in which many of Blossom's friends seemed to feature was *"Kite,"* the literary magazine mentioned earlier.

Although ostensibly for employees' contributions only, there were so many notable persons included in some editions that it is hard to imagine that they worked in the factory in any capacity at all. Blossom's input, in whatever way she was instrumental in it, is shown in a photograph of her in the *"Miles Magazine"* with the caption: "Mrs F.G. Miles seated before the microphone reads her script in French to open the *'Kite'* broadcast." Blossom is looking very relaxed and smiling: she is the only one of the five in the picture who is, the others look tense to a high degree . . .

"Kite" is, or has become, extremely obscure. There are only three of its editions still known to archivists, only one of these being numbered, that headed No.5, Spring 1946. One of the others says in the editorial: "This is the fourth issue of *'Kite,'* the first in peace-time." In what looks like the first edition, the editor, A.R. Rose, is only twenty-three years old and a draughtsman, but he says in another magazine that the first edition was printed from type-written stencils and stapled together by hand, so it is not clear whether this was republished in the form in which it survives or not. In this same publication he *[presumably A.R. Rose]* writes that the authors include:

" . . . draughtsmen, wood workers, progress chasers, perhaps fifteen in all. This may not seem like many out of the thousands of Miles employees but when you think about it a fair proportion of writers for an engineering community. Of these an A.I.D. inspector called Alan Griffiths, the author of several novels and one-time contributor to *"Punch"* was the only one who had been a professional man of letters prewar. Mrs Miles, now President of the Circle, came along, armed like the rest with a manuscript. I knew at once from the atmosphere that the idea had clicked. Since then we have been meeting every few weeks after work, reading our stories to each other and exchanging comments, with restraint at first, later with brutal frankness. We published *"Kite"* number one in April 1944, christening it after the aeroplanes which had brought us together. We were given a loan of ten pounds to launch us on the way to literary fame and fortune . . . Fortunately all seven hundred [copies] were sold within two

149

days. We paid back the loan with a flourish and . . . lodged ten shillings in the bank. . . ."

Then last September we received a letter from the B.B.C., one of whose producers had bought a copy by chance from a shop in Charing Cross Road.

'We have,' she wrote, 'in the French Service, a weekly feature called "Angleterre en Mouvement" where, in feature form, we deal with all subjects that can be rather vaguely classed as 'progressive.' For example Sir William Beveridge has spoken on Social Security, Eleanor Rathbone on Family Allowances.

I very much wondered whether it would be possible to do something about the factory where the contributors for "Kite" work.'

We knew of only one answer to that proposition. After collecting together a few people who could speak French or were willing to try, I wrote a script which, translated and cut to shape, was broadcast on two occasions.

Several contributors took part including Mrs Miles, on whom we have always been able to depend for support. Her introduction to 'Kite' Number Three, delivered on the occasion in French, provided the keynote to the whole programme. Quoting from the original, here is a part of what she said:

' . . . there is still a widespread idea that a factory is a place quite apart from your real life where you get your work done as quickly and as well as you can and brush the dust off your heels as soon as your job is finished. But these days factories are more and more inclined to take on the character of a community and those who work there begin to find interests in common outside the day to day manufacturing work. The 'Kite' is the expression of some of the literary interests of the factory. The enthusiasts who have come together to create this paper have undoubtedly got a great deal of enjoyment out of it for themselves but a far greater number have had the enjoyment of reading what they have written. I think and hope it may have encouraged others to try their hand at authorship.

For our part we should like to add that the community characteristic referred to is particularly strong in Miles

Aircraft and we believe that this has contributed largely to whatever success 'Kite' had has enjoyed so far.

Meanwhile we have another issue in preparation. We are looking for yet more writers in every industrial trade and profession to make it the most representative and entertaining collection yet. With their help we will keep the 'Kite' flying.'"

Among contributors to "Kite" are Hans Keller, who was to become famous as a musicologist, violinist, violist, composer and critic, working with Benjamin Britten and a doyen of "The Listener" and the B.B.C. He was another of Blossom's refugees. Born in Vienna, a Jew but with some Irish blood, he was imprisoned during the *anschluss* but escaped and fled to Britain. From the middle of the fifties his musical theories included that of functional analysis, designed to identify the single unifying idea from which a whole composition is derived. He claimed complete objectivity for his musical demonstrations, some of which were broadcast. His piece in "Kite," a rather strange story called "Don Juan Again" seems to be about disillusioned love, but might be about something entirely different, as in the biographical notes on 'New Contributors' it states: "HANS KELLER . . . His activities are three-fold: psychological (his first scientific book is just going to press), musical (L.R.A.M. violin) and literary. At present working with Margaret Phillips ("The Education of the Emotions") on research in group psychology."

It is hard to see that he could also be working in the factory: maybe Blossom found a post for him. It was a tragic irony that another Hans (Hannes) Keller was to have such a terrible impact on the family a few years hence.

A 'New Contributor' to the Spring 1946 edition was the established writer Elizabeth Taylor. She was a highly-regarded novelist of serious fiction and is still read and published today. It has been impossible to find out how or why she wrote for "Kite," or whether she knew Blossom personally. She went to the Abbey School in Reading and her husband was in the R.A.F. stationed at Shinfield Park. They lived in Caversham for some time and then in High Wycombe, so any of these factors could have led to her introduction to Blossom; but it seems unlikely that she fulfilled the criterion for writing for *"Kite"* by actually being a worker. This story called "Ever So Banal" was hitherto unknown in her bibliography.

In the March 1946 issue of the *"News"* Blossom notes in her editorial under a letter from A.R. Rose about *"Kite"* that this "reminds us to offer hearty congratulations to Anthony and Mrs Rose upon the birth of their first son."

She also includes a note: "Will the member of the Shops who lent me a specimen of embroidery (showing the Miles Hawk) a few weeks ago please be good enough to come and see me again – M. Miles." These personal touches enliven the publication at a time when the economic future looked uncertain, if not distinctly bleak.

One of the many notable and interesting personalities who stayed with Blossom and F.G. during their Woodley years was Cecil Lewis. He had been one of the five founding employees of the B.B.C. (only five applied for the post!) and, later, commercial television. He must have been quite a difficult house guest; he and his wife *had* to stay at Lands End House because he had sold his own house to buy a Gemini from his "good friend Miles," in which to fly to South Africa in the autumn of 1947.

Not only was he enmeshed in the philosophy of Gurdjieff (a bizarre mixture of self-assessment and self-knowledge based on a lot of difficult dance sequences and poses and a disruptive life-style) but also he was – to quote his own autobiography – possessed of "a gargantuan sexual appettite" and spent much time trying to seduce F.G.'s and Blossom's secretary Joan Ellis, later Joan Angell, writing love poetry to her and leaving it in her office if she was out, while his second wife Olga was less than a mile away. He is quite frank about himself saying that sex "was a problem for him" and that "seducers make bad husbands" and "everybody lies about sex."

His friendship with Blossom and F.G. went back to the days of the B.B.C. radio and during the war he returned to the R.A.F., having been a flyer in the first World War when only in his teens, and was re-taught to fly at Woodley with No.8 E.F.T.S. He was afterwards stationed at Booker and rented a cottage close by. His philosophy echoed that of Dr Tibor Csato in some respects.

He is mainly remembered for his book *"Sagitarius Rising"* which is a classic, but he wrote many books, some novels and

"Gemini to Joburg," an account of the journey he and Olga made to South Africa to found a Gurdjieff colony. It was a tribute to the Miles Gemini that they made it without serious injury and not too much in the way of disaster. He could not afford, he said, to have the 'searchlight' (landing light) installed in the Gemini, and trying to land in the dark on remote Greek and African strips in 1947 was not to be recommended, but he made it several times.

The Gemini was sold when he eventually found a suitable site for the 'Colony' (which soon proved not to be suitable at all) for £100 more than he paid for it.

The journey started in typical fashion; having taken off from Woodley, Olga declared that she had left her make-up case behind and that she just had to have it; so having landed at Lympne on the coast he returned to Woodley to get her make-up – well, there was only another 6,000 miles to go! Nevertheless Cecil was "furious." He describes Olga as a "dainty little thing," half Burmese and half French. Their marriage didn't survive "Gurdjieff" in the long term. The Gemini was an ideal aircraft for such a project, indeed, for any project, and Geminis were owned and flown by such personalities as Prince Bira and Sir Douglas Bader; several are still flying today or being rebuilt.

CHAPTER 9

POSTWAR PROBLEMS

In 1947 F.G. received what he called "one of the worst shocks I have ever had in my life."

Great Britain was, at that time, deep into many crises, the main trouble being the fuel shortage. There were other shortages: materials, food, every sort of consumer goods, but the fuel problem compounded all the others.

Money was another government headache: restrictions on the importation of materials and things like engines especially affected all sort of industries, particularly aircraft manufacturers. Foreign currency was restricted then and for many years to come. Even by 1951 the overseas travel allowance per person was only £26 per annum. Many foods were still rationed in 1952, so in 1947 there was a long way to go. With great timing the winter of 1947 was one of the worst in recent history. Prolonged persistent frost meant the landscape was encased in clear ice for months and road surfaces were broken up and dangerous, and when the thaw did eventually come serious flooding added to everyone's misery.

The government evidently had no alternative to the fuel crisis but to issue an edict closing down all factories and similar establishments for a period of three weeks.

The first issue of *"News"* for 1947 was still on a fairly cheerful theme of New Year's greetings, with thoughts from F.G. and George Miles and Sir William Mount, who by then had joined the Board. F.G. is writing in terms of "cautious confidence" and "sound commercial additions to the solidarity of the firm." He mentions having just introduced the shorter working week (then an innovative measure of 42½ hours on a five-day basis) and claims that: "If anyone can say where in the world there is a better chance of happy industrial relationships, good employment, a good standard of living conditions, and a full life *[than at Miles Aircraft]*, then I for one should find it hard to believe him." He says he is confident at

154

achieving targets and that "1947 will prove to be our best and greatest year."

That was "*News*" Volume 6, No.1. By Volume 6 No.2 the headline is: "A 'BACKS-TO-THE-WALL' MESSAGE."

Under this title F.G. begins:

"As you all know, I have just come back from the United States and from South America, where we have big potential markets for our newest products: for the Merchantman, the Marathon and all the other things besides aeroplanes that we are making.

When I was in Argentina I had the first news of the shut-down. Afterwards I had a letter from my wife, which gave me the full details. It was one of the worst shocks I have ever had in my life.

The plans we had made before I went away – plans not only for this year but for two or even three years ahead – were sound . . . I was able to say that this firm was as solid as any firm could be. We had plenty of orders, we were in production, we had everything . . . to allow us to look forward to prosperity for all of us."

He goes on to explain the full implications of the shutdown and its lasting and ongoing effects: shortages, supply interruptions, shedding electricity loads etc., and continues bitterly:

"I am sure you realise that America has some very definite opinions about us. While I was there, I met many good and influential friends; *every one of them was sure that England is finished and ended.* Everyone of them believes that this is a jam we can never get out of. They consider that no one who is fighting for life itself, as Britain has been doing, could stand a month of shut-down in industry."

Of course he exhorts all to make a supreme effort and asks everyone to do "about 7½% to 10% more work" as "we cannot afford waiting time, slackness, wanderers, prolonged tea-breaks or waste. These are luxuries neither we, nor Britain, can stomach today. If you look around and see a little of this, you will know we are winning. If you see a lot, we are losing." His final paragraph would not have gone down well with the workforce who were already losing money by the shutdown.

In the next issue, in April 1947, James McCutcheon "follows up the message from Mr F.G. Miles in the March issue." This looks rather like damage limitation as F.G.'s words might have seemed somewhat ill-chosen, and McCutcheon explains the economic situation on a national level with regard to imports and exports.

Then, curiously, he says: "For many years workers have had antagonisms to what has been commonly called the Capitalist system," and he too sees that: "everyone can assist by doing that little bit extra"; this seems naive humbug to us today, but was believed at the time. He continues: "It is only by the sum of the local effort that the national problem can be solved. We must not allow ourselves to be blinded by the propaganda that increased effort will only produce greater profit for the few." He finishes quite a long dissertation with the words: "Governments, Industrialists, Managements, Trades Unions, *you and I* all have an important part to play. Yet always (and in conclusion) we must not forget that "All work and no play . . . " *[the capitals and punctuation are his]*.

There is no doubt, in hindsight, that this shutdown was the beginning of the end as far as Miles Aircraft was concerned. There were other factors like the excess profit tax and the unsophisticated accounting system that Miles employed, but the national shutdown produced a cash-flow situation to which there was no solution.

The innovative approach that F.G. and Blossom had to technical products resulted in several really advanced inventions taking their place on the production lines. Any one of these should have resulted in prosperity on a long-term and grand scale.

Work on classified secret weapons like the directional stability facility for air-launched torpedos led to other projects. Miles had designed the equivalent to the German flying bomb ("Doodlebug") which caused so much terror as early as 1941. These projects led on to an auto-pilot system. The Miles electric actuator was also a by-product of the research, as were many other navigational and training aids, but two things more than any others which should have made a huge fortune for all involved were the Biro ball-point pen and the Copycat copier.

It is difficult to imagine life without either of these very common items today. Ball-point pens are now so cheap that they are given away as advertising material – the first ones cost the equivalent of a week's wages.

Lazlo Biro was originally from Hungary but had taken Argentinian citizenship; F.G. saw the potential of his invention as early as 1944 and the development of the pen was carried out at Woodley in great secrecy. At first F.G. saw the project as being only really of use to pilots or mariners where writing by conventional means was difficult or impossible because of reduced air pressure or very wet conditions. By 1947 students at Miles Aeronautical School were being given the first examples of Biros to "see how they worked," which they did very badly initially. Many students' notes were obscured by streaks and blobs from the experimental pens, sometimes even with red ink, and there were many production problems, mainly with the ink flow. However the snags were eventually ironed out and the ball-point pen was launched to an amazed world.

Another advance of almost science-fictional proportions was the Copycat, a photostatic copying machine developed by the Head of the Photographic Department. This was received by F.G. with so much enthusiasm that it became almost an offence to take a carbon copy of a letter! But the commercial development of the photocopier (as we know it today) came too late to save Miles from economic extinction.

While the financial crisis deepened Blossom was still dedicating much of her time to the welfare of her workforce. In July 1947 she decribes the works library thus:

"BOOKS? – YES, 5,000!
With a total of more than five thousand books in circulation and on the shelves, our Works Library provides a mental meal which could be more than a little indigestible for the diner unused to such rich and varied food for thought."

She goes on:

"Thrillers of the 'Oo dun it?' variety are in and out every day, but the more thoughtful type of reading has an ever increasing interest."

A librarian was engaged and "the best of each batch" of newly-published books were bought. She remarks on the statistic that "strangely enough, in March and at Christmas-time, . . . the average *[of books borrowed]* falls sharply."

In July 1947, too, Britain (and the world) was trying to get back to normality. The Reading Aero Club reopened with a couple of refurbished prewar Miles Hawk Trainers, which had survived the war with the R.A.F. An Aerovan and a Gemini provided trips to the seaside, the Aeronautical School staged its sports day in Palmer Park and Miles Aircraft held its Open Day on the 20th. Blossom did not write the article about the Open Day but it is worth recording that the headline above it was "Into Miles Aircraft Strode the Ten Thousand."

The idea was mooted of a new sports ground for Miles, and an Extraordinary General Meeting of the sports club members was held on July 30th with great forward-looking plans and estimates and soil analysis for bowling greens, tennis courts, two football grounds, two cricket pitches, a hockey ground and a netball pitch. With the headline "New Sports Ground to be One of the Best in the South of England" the *"Works Magazine"* continued:

> "There is also space for other activities. Provision is to be made for a suitable pavilion immediately building restrictions permit, and, in the meantime, hut accommodation, licensed if possible, would be provided."

The site was to be Sonning Lane. It was another forty years before this site did indeed become a sports ground under the aegis of the Reading Cricket and Hockey Club.

A proposal was made outlining the suggested organisation for a Miles Model Engineering Society; a photograph of a beautiful Bugatti was included and mention of a model of the Queen Mary excited interest, as did the Miles Aircraft Horticultural Society and the Miles Aircraft Works Band.

By June 1947 the variety of activities going on was remarkable. There were full reports of cricket matches, inter-departmental and outside; the Angling Club held its annual dinner, and many prizes were awarded, including the "F.G. Miles Cup" and the "Mrs F.G. Miles Rod"; the Miles Aircraft Rifle Club entered teams in the Industrial League; the Sky Observers Club met in a German aircraft, a Junkers 52, donated by Blossom; the Boxing Section held their AGM; the Minor Football Club line-up was photographed by the Miles Aircraft Camera Club; the second Walter Capley Scholarship winner was announced; and it seems that the purchase of fourteen acres for the Sports Field in Holme Park, Sonning had actually gone ahead for £2,000.

The Miles Golfing Society flourished; the Royal Aeronautical Society announced that their Garden Party was to be held at Woodley in September; the Technical School held an Open Day with students organising an "interesting Static Exhibition" and a Boys' Gymnastic Display, and the girls evidently impressed all and sundry with "skipping to music"!

The Joint Production Committee met to discuss and sort out production problems, mentioning bad weather, dock strikes and "other labour troubles."

By September 1947 we have "Farewell to the 'News'" as outlined in the previous chapter on Blossom's editorials and her writings. It is always darkest before the dawn. Most clichés are profound: in 1947, for Blossom and F.G. the dawn seemed to precede the darkness.

It was hard, with so many projects in the pipeline and even more in F.G.'s and Blossom's minds, to see the decline and fall of the company come about through totally financial trauma.

We should recognise that in the future the aircraft industry was to become so complex and so technically esoteric that no small or medium-size firm was ultimately to survive. Even the great personality of Sir Frederick Handley Page, who held out against amalgamation longer than most, was not enough to save that venerable manufacturing company from eventually going under. Amalgamation followed amalgamation nationally and then internationally as costs skyrocketed and prices went into the stratosphere.

However in 1947 and 1948 no one could foresee the degree of the scientific and industrial changes ahead. F.G. became very bitter, as he was entitled to, having worked so hard for the good of the country, the company and his workers. Blossom had to remain outwardly serenely acceptant and this is the beginning of her severely-disciplined manner remembered by those who knew her in later years.

In March 1947 a prospectus had been issued in good faith as the number of orders looked as if they would provide a secure year ahead, in spite of the severity of the problems caused by the weather and the country's economy. This prospectus was to prove a pivotal point in the proceedings which were later brought against F.G.

How hard it must have been for F.G. and Blossom not only to lose the company that they had built up but for that to result in the terrifying blow of F.G. being tried at the Old Bailey for misrepresentation in a case brought by three shareholders.

In November 1947 F.G. had written of "a terrible shock . . . found it suddenly impossible to obtain any information . . . I was not consulted . . . I could not get help . . . an atmosphere of secrecy . . . my being asked . . . to keep away from the factory . . . The factory is in a state of sullen bewilderment."

Many words have been written, some contradictory, regarding the causes of the collapse of the firm. Many thousands of local people were affected, many local residents who did not even work at Miles were deeply saddened; Miles Aircraft had been a symbol of something very special. It was difficult to see it as a symptom of postwar economics because it had such a personal basis, and blame was savagely apportioned by workers and well-wishers alike, and none of this blame was directed against F.G. and Blossom – far from it.

The fact that the case against F.G. was dismissed after a trial lasting seventeen days did not alleviate the intense distress felt by him and Blossom, especially as, although he was fully acquitted, he still had to pay costs, his share of which was about £20,000, a massive sum at that time. This trial did not take place until May 1950, so the worry and apprehension had been on their minds for more than two years.

Blossom's beloved students and her Aeronautical School were taken over temporarily by Reading Education Authority so that the students could complete their course examinations for A.F.R.Ae.S or A.M.I.Mech.E. qualifications, but the Authority insisted that the partially complete Venture aeroplane should be broken up and destroyed and this was done by the students themselves with a sledgehammer and very mixed feelings. The final intake of students left in July 1949 and the buildings of the school were used as farm stores, warehouses, Tupperware depositories, waste dumps etc. until they were finally demolished in 1990 to make way for an extension for the vast housing estate that by then occupied Woodley Airfield. The Robin hangar alone, in which the Venture was built, was saved from destruction and now forms the nucleus of the Museum of Berkshire Aviation although on a different site, one quite close to the old hostel of Sandford Manor, which still survives.

Not only did F.G. and Blossom have to leave Woodley and Miles Aircraft but they also had to leave Lands End House, the house and home designed so lovingly by themselves and with such high hopes only a few years before.

*   *   *

Sir Johnston was still remembered in 1948 when a bust of him was unveiled at Drury Lane Theatre. He was in good company because a bust of Shakespeare was unveiled at the same time. Sir John Gielgud unveiled Shakespeare while Peter Forbes-Robertson, Johnston's grand-nephew, unveiled his. It was a statuette that had been hanging around the theatre for some time, having been presented by Frank Forbes-Robertson who was dead by then. The bust was repositioned on the first floor of the rotunda.

Blossom's mother died on Christmas Eve 1950 at St. Margaret's Bay. There was a report of her death in *"The Times"* on December 27th and then an obituary and appreciation on December 28th. The headline was "An Appealing Actress" and the gist of the tribute was that she had charm but in a limited range of acting. She was always to be in the shadow of both her magnetic sister and her illustrious husband.

For Blossom it was just another blow at a time when she already had too many problems to cope with, and the fact that it was Christmas Eve was just a portent of more tragic twists of fate to come.

With Blossom's heredity and environmental set-backs it is a total mystery how she was able to maintain her supreme air of calm acceptance and serenity. Her maternal grandmother had suffered mental problems resulting in her being confined, her father had

161

had a breakdown of some severity. Her finely-honed artistic temperament was not one of stout, sluggish indifference. She cared so deeply for the poor, the dispossessed. She not only cared but tried to alleviate the hardships that others endured. When her sister Chloe died so young, it affected her deeply. The death of Tony Wilding was another blow in her youth. The tension that existed all her life between her father and her Aunt Maxine hung about the air like a black cloud, terrifying her mother and putting a strain on the girls from their infancy.

All creative geniuses agonise over the part they play in their particular field. Frank Whittle had more than one nervous breakdown in his quest to develop the jet engine; Vincent Van Gogh, Edward Elgar, John Ogden, Jacqueline Duprez – arts as well as sciences produced their martyrs. Art and engineering went hand in hand in Blossom's life, both adding their stresses and strains and yet, when one met her, she appeared as if she had not a care in the world and furthermore never had had a care.

CHAPTER 10

LIFE (AND DEATH) IN SUSSEX

In December 1948 F.G. Miles Ltd. was set up on Redhill aerodrome in Surrey, and Blossom took a back seat as far as aviation was concerned. F.G. took especial interest in electronics and its potential, and in structural plastics. Whereas all through the forties F.G. never ceased to write articles and letters to the newspapers on many subjects including postwar aviation, the employment of blind people in industry, on passenger aeroplanes of the future, on state control of the aircraft industry and his forthright views on aerodromes, during the fifties he became strangely silent.

Then in 1951 the wheel finally turned full circle. As Tim Webb's book, *"Shoreham Airport, Sussex,"* describes it:

"In mid-1951 Miles began his return to Shoreham with a nucleus of his design staff. On October 1st 1951 Grahame Gates arrived at Shoreham after being invited to join the team as Chief Project Designer, and in January 1952 George Miles came from Airspeeds to rejoin his brother at Shoreham. History had once more repeated itself with another member of the Gates family working at Shoreham and the Miles brothers back where they started . . ."

Towards the end of the fifties F.G. revived his interest in film archives and was instrumental in getting a copy of a silent film screened in which his late father-in-law took the main part, and, indeed approached Mr Ernest Lundgren, who was then curator of the National Film Archives, to get it deposited there and catalogued, preserved and available for showing.

A report in *"The Times"* in April 1960 headed by a large still photograph from this film stated that:

"This silent film of 1913 shown at the National Film Theatre brings back a great Hamlet. Sir Johnston Forbes-Robertson was past sixty when the film was shot. The performance is a

163

resurrection astonishing in its vigour. It is thanks to Mr F.G. Miles, a son-in-law of Forbes-Robertson, that this valuable link in the tradition of heroic acting is now restored. The copy is one reissued by Gaumont in the early 1920s probably with cuts."

There is reference to the only other archive of Forbes-Robertson being "an unsatisfactory gramophone record" and the article goes on: "Robert Atkins, a subdued Marcellus, reappears as a dashing Player King. Mr Atkins remembers working on location for the film at Lulworth Cove in Dorset."

Although it is hard to think that something as essentially verbal as Shakespeare could have been satisfactorily conveyed in a silent film "with very few subtitles" the power of Sir Johnston's acting was summed up by the *"Times"* critic saying: "One has rarely witnessed such stoical loneliness."

This report prompted a letter from Mrs Dorothy E. Thompson of Watford in *"The Times"* on May 3rd 1960:

> "I was interested to read in *"The Times"* of April 25th about the existing silent film of Forbes-Robertson as Hamlet. I was fortunate as a girl to be taken to see this great actor's production of the play. Once seen his Hamlet could never be forgotten. I have seen others but he is unrivalled. His beautiful voice . . ."

She says that the supreme moment was the "Get thee to a nunnery" passage:

> "Ophelia, played by Mrs Patrick Campbell, looking too old for the part, her face buried in her hands, could not see what the audience could," *[which was Hamlet standing behind her conveying such emotion that it was]* "a poignant memory still." *[This was after maybe fifty years or more. As an interesting footnote she goes on:]* "When the curtain had fallen on the stage tragedy we heard of one that had been enacted in reality for it was the night William Terris was murdered while entering his theatre."

*   *   *

George Miles became the prime mover in the Company set up at their old airfield at Shoreham. He developed many of his innovative ideas there and some of them were successful, but always the lack of capital finance was to hinder real progress on a grand scale. Nevertheless he continued to be an influence in aircraft manufacture (and the spin-offs from this industry) for many years into his eighties when he was still a consultant.

Jeremy continued at Harrow and later became a pilot in the Fleet Air Arm; he was also to play a part with George in the experimental aircraft developed at Shoreham. Some of their employees from Woodley loyally followed them to Redhill and then Shoreham and remained with them right to the end.

It may be an exaggeration to say that F.G. was "a broken man" after the betrayal and perfidy he had endured with the loss of his firm and the court case which followed it, but certainly he was bitter and could not accept or come to terms with his feelings. Because Blossom had to be the strong one in the relationship, then that is what she became; and she later had to accept her blindness in much the same spirit.

The event which finally broke F.G. was so terrible that it is impossible to imagine how Blossom ever survived it.

*   *   *

Mary, Blossom's daughter, was making a career as a photographer and met Peter Small, a journalist. He was twelve years older than her but she fell deeply in love with him and they were married at the Register Office in Worthing, Peter having previously been married and divorced. Mary's address at the time of the marriage was given as the Sussex Yacht Club, Shoreham which may have sounded slightly strange, but Peter's address had an even more curious ring to it as it was Hamilton Terrace, London, NW8, as had been Blossom's and her husband, Inigo Freeman-Thomas, at the time of her first marriage. Aunt Maxine can hardly have been exerting her posthumous influence this time as Peter's father was a fish-fryer and obviously not one of Aunt Maxine's nobility. Was it just a coincidence?

Blossom was a witness together with Bernard Eaton, and F.G. still gave his occupation as an aircraft designer. Mary and Peter were married on 3rd September 1962.

Peter Small was not only a journalist but very involved with science and scientific experiments in underwater techniques. He

165

was very well-known and is still remembered today by the members of sub-aqua clubs all over the world.

In October 1962 an article written by Peter appeared in *"The Times."* The subject was underwater exploration. As a photographer, Mary was also interested in this comparatively new sport and the opportunities it provided. Even today sub-aquatic sports are one of the most dangerous, many times more lethal than amateur boxing, with two hundred and twenty deaths per million underwater hours; in 1962 it was even more so. Not long after they were married Mary and Peter both went to the United States and the progression of the story is evident in the following reports which appeared in *"The Times"*:

"THE TIMES"
December 5th 1962

TWO BRITONS DIE IN DIVING ATTEMPT
from our own correspondent
New York Dec. 4 1962

Two Britons died yesterday in an attempt to set up a new skin-diving record on LONG BEACH, CALIFORNIA. The two men, Mr Peter Small, aged 35, a journalist, and Mr Christopher Whittaker, aged 22, a geology student at California University, were taking part in an experiment with Mr Hannes Keller, the Swiss skin-diver, who had claimed the world's diving record of 728 ft.

Mr Keller and Mr Small were lowered 1,000 ft beneath the surface in a diving bell. Both men were wearing frogmen's suits and carried air tanks filled with a mixture of gases devised by Mr Keller as a means of enabling man to survive the intense pressure experienced at such depths.

Evidently something went wrong in the chamber, for a television camera lowered alongside it disclosed that both men had collapsed.

WENT TO HELP
Mr Whittaker went down with another man to assist as the diving bell was brought slowly to the surface, but vanished under water. His body has not so far been recovered. Mr Keller and Mr

Small were given treatment on the surface but Mr Small was dead on arrival at Long Beach Hospital. It was stated today that Mr Keller has recovered.

Both Mr Small and Mr Keller were suffering from the "bends" – the explosion of nitrogen bubbles in the blood caused by external pressure and lack of oxygen. It is this which Mr Keller's formula of gases, which he keeps secret, is designed to overcome.

"THE TIMES"
January 5th 1963

Mr Small – inventor absolved from criminal negligence.

"THE TIMES"
February 13th 1963

SKIN DIVER'S WIDOW FOUND DEAD IN FLAT

Mrs Mary Small, aged 23, widow of the journalist and skin-diver, Mr Peter Small, who died in a diving accident off California in December, was found dead yesterday in a room full of gas in her flat in Duke Street, W. Mrs Small was the daughter of Mr F.G. Miles, the aircraft designer.

"THE TIMES"
February 20th 1963

SKIN DIVER'S WIDOW WAS DEPRESSED

Mrs Mary Small, widow of Peter Small, the skin-diver, had many photographs of herself and her husband about a foot away from her head on the carpet, police said at the inquest on Mrs Small in London yesterday.

Mrs Small, aged 23, was found dead in her flat in Duke Street Mansions, Duke Street, Mayfair. A gas tap was on. Mr Gavin Thurston, the Westminster Coroner, said: "I shall record that she died from carbon monoxide poisoning, self-adminstered while she was suffering from reactive depression.

Mrs Small was with her husband when he died in an attempt to reach a record depth of 1,000 ft in a diving bell off the California coast last December.

Mrs Diana Sheean, a writer and aunt of Mrs Small, said: "After Peter's death the reaction was perhaps the most normal you could imagine in that she was absolutely broken-hearted but not frozen up – she would weep and weep and weep."

Such insupportable grief! No human being could be expected to endure so much suffering. She was entitled to end the torture. In the days when domestic gas was poisonous, a sudden impulse was enough. It was so easy, quick and painless, even pleasurable, I believe. There was no planning involved, no other person need be implicated, and considerations of the family members being left behind could be overcome by the thought that their suffering could be relieved as well by being rid of the ongoing reminder of the tragedy which provoked the action.

I do not know the statistics of such deaths but in my own family, in one year alone, three of my relations chose this way to end their lives.

For Blossom it was a double, even triple, tragedy. In any such similar situations the mother of the family always blames herself. Hindsight is a terrible weapon. We can say that life was never going to be the same again for Blossom. F.G. was affected physically and the damage was cumulative with his other business problems. Blossom seemed able to rely on inner stores of strength but this was only on the surface and for the outside world to see. So . . . life went on.

For Blossom the end of 1962 and the beginning of 1963 tested her serenity and discipline. After the death of her son-in-law in such unnecessarily tragic circumstances at the beginning of December "The Times" reported on December 19th:

"Miss Jean Forbes-Robertson, the actress, who has been in Charing Cross Hospital for a week, was said by a hospital spokesman to be still seriously ill."

And then on December 27th it carried the headline: "Barrie's Favourite Peter Pan" and the following obituary:

"Miss Jean Forbes-Robertson (Mrs André Van Gyseghem) the actress died on Christmas Eve at the age of fifty seven. Her early work had been all that was expected of a daughter of Sir

Johnston Forbes-Robertson and his American-born wife, Gertrude Elliot, and that was a great deal. But having quickly reached the front rank in her profession she dropped out of it and she brought her career in the theatre to a premature end before she was fifty. . . . the second of her parents' three daughters, [Chloe was already dead by then] went to school at Heathfield, Ascot and first appeared professionally in her mother's company – her father having already retired – in South Africa in 1921. With such surprising talent she found herself at twenty-two heir to all the good will of her septuagenarian father."

There was an inset of a small photograph of her in profile as Peter Pan, the Forbes-Robertson features much in evidence. It continued:

"During the second World War she and André Van Gyseghem, her second husband, her first marriage to Mr Hamish Hamilton the publisher having been dissolved, toured with their own company and with The Old Vic. There was a daughter of her marriage to Mr André Van Gyseghem."

Her funeral took place at St. Mary's, Bryanston Square, and those attending included Sir Lewis Casson and Dame Sybil Thorndike, Mr and Mrs Mark Dignam, as well as the family members, husband and daughter, Joanna, Blossom and F.G., her sister Diana, her Aunt Ida Forbes-Robertson and, poignantly, niece Mrs P. Small.

No wonder that Mary finally became too depressed to go on, with so much death in the forefront; then Blossom had to endure another funeral, that of her only daughter, Mary.

* * *

By now Blossom was living at Batts, Ashurst, near Steyning in West Sussex. Ten years went by; they go quicker when one is older and the period seemed much shorter to Blossom than the glory years of Miles Aircraft at Woodley. She retained such equanimity that all who knew her during this period remarked upon the fact.

F.G. formed another company jointly with Societé de Construction des Avions Hurel-Dubois to market an aircraft outwardly similar to the Aerovan but with a wing of very high aspect ratio. There were to be several projected versions of this design but it never went into production and the design was eventually sold to Short Brothers to become the basis for the Short Skyvan.

When Blossom and F.G. left Woodley they first went to Redhill, as has already been mentioned; there they continued the aircraft business in a small way for a while, and lived in a very nice house. There seemed to be no diminution in their lifestyle, due probably to the legacy of Aunt Maxine. They next moved to Rustington which is on the coast near Littlehampton, but they were able to sell this house and land for development to achieve a more tranquil and satisfying home at Ashurst. While they were waiting for their house "Batts" to be built they lived on their boat, the "Mary Susannah," in Shoreham harbour, and indeed Mary was to be married from this location, but that was much later. The faithful Jan who had been with them since 1949 when he had been smuggled out of Latvia in a laundry basket came into his own as an impressive steward on the boat.

The village of Ashurst in Sussex is hardly more than a hamlet, it is so small and so tucked away. Nevertheless it is a village because it has a beautiful little twelfth century Church and a school and, of course, the statutory pub. On Christopher Saxon's map of the 1570s it is obvious why Ashurst remained cut off, being hemmed in on three sides by rivers and on the fourth side by the Downs and meandering streams; the area around the church cannot have changed much since the sixteenth century. Even today the remnants of an old rickety bridge betray its ancient access route, the old bridleway from Henfield. We must not call "The Fountain" the "statutory pub," its noblest description is in *"The Four Men"* by Hilaire Belloc:

> "The Fountain of Ashurst runs, by God's grace with better stuff
> than water . . . For though there are honourable years around
> the Fountain of Ashurst, yet certainly there are no regrets. It is
> not done for yet. Binge! Fountain, binge!"

In 1902 Belloc made the pilgrimage on foot across Sussex from east to west and his book sums up the magical atmosphere still to be found there today, because I made the journey myself eighty-seven years later.

When Blossom and F.G. moved to Batts at Ashurst it almost looked as if they were hiding from the world and perhaps they were. Batts is an interesting house and the reason for this is that the architect, Mr Russell, won an award for its design. He still lives in the village and it is typical of Blossom that she should have been involved in encouraging two young architects in two houses she owned. The house is up a short private driveway, not a large house but not a small one either. It was not far from Shoreham where F.G. intended to continue his career and, of course, it could not really be so remote as it seems when one is there, being only a short distance from such busy centres as Brighton, Eastbourne, Worthing and other popular coastal resorts, but as it was built on the site of a much older farmhouse, retaining part of two of the old walls, the ambience is of the lonely seclusion of the countryside.

When they bought the site, most of the old farmhouse was already in decay and so it was a blank canvas with which David Russell could work. At first the architect suggested to F.G. a building of glass and timber and he was enthusiastic, but Blossom said: "No, I want a Georgian house." She pointed out that, as she was brought up in the Georgian splendour of Bedford Square, she wanted a house to echo her memories of No.22. David Russell carried out her wishes to such a dedicated degree that a few years later Sussex County heritage department confirmed it as of the Georgian period, listed it for preservation and argued with the architect, insisting that it was indeed built in 1750! It is now listed in its own right as a beautiful building.

Although it has only five or six bedrooms plus dressing rooms and bathrooms it looks imposing both inside and out. Wherever possible designs and some materials of circa 1750 were employed. Comfort and design met in the underfloor electric heating so that the interiors would not be marred by intrusive radiators: even the upstairs bathrooms had underfloor heating. The extensive grounds were controlled by a ha-ha to eliminate fencing. The swimming pool was overlooked by a Michael Ayrton sculpture and F.G. taught all the village children to swim in the pool.

About this time we have yet another change of names: F.G. was known as "Psah" (although the spelling of this is dubious) and Blossom became "Blossie."

"Psah" continued his innovative ways with designs and inventions including a crab-like mechanism to clean swimming pools. Tested on his own swimming pool, the prototype sometimes took in water resulting in spectacular explosions and fortuitous fountains. He also supplied the plastic pillars which adorned the genuine 1750 portico.

The peace and tranquillity was shattered by the death of Mary, as previously documented. Her fateful last weekend had been spent at Batts and Blossom tried to persuade her to stay at Batts on the Sunday night. Mary insisted on driving back to her flat in London and Joan Angell, ringing up just after Mary had left, asked Blossom with the deep concern that all her friends felt: "How is Mary?" Blossom said: "She's fine, really fine, she is doing well, she wouldn't stay the night, she wanted to get home." Just a few hours after that conversation, Mary was dead. Blossom agonised over not persuading her more forcefully to stay over. Mrs Margery Cobby who worked for Blossom on a part-time basis considered that Blossom never got over this tragedy, but architect David Russell said that she showed the typical English 'stiff upper lip' attitude and it was difficult to interpret her true feelings. Joan Angell agreed with David Russell.

Blossom never wanted staff to 'live in' and so even the general factotum Jan lived in a nearby cottage and arrived for work everyday at 6 am. There was a bungalow in the grounds where the gardener lived; after he retired, Blossom never took on another gardener. The nanny, "Nonny," did live in at first, a room being specially designed for her, but later Blossom bought a cottage for her.

Business ventures at Shoreham appeared succesful; Prince Philip visited their set-up and such VIPs as the chairman of Shell gave the projects a firm basis but F.G. was beginning to show signs of the arterial disease which was to disable him.

Eventually the arteriosclerosis was to become so severe that although "Psah" tried to continue working on his archives in his workroom which was housed outside the house at Batts, he became so confused that Blossom reluctantly agreed that he should go into a nursing home, "Larkspur," in Hewling Way, Worthing. Once again Blossom showed the 'stiff upper lip' syndrome. She employed

Joan Angell (who had been F.G.'s and her own secretary from the war years onward, and who had married Jack Angell and actually lived in the cottage opposite Batts, before Jack went to South Africa and afterwards moved to Shoreham Beach) to reorganise and annotate all his files and data. These seem to have disappeared after Blossom's death.

F.G. died on August 15th 1976.

He was only seventy-three, but the causes of death were given as Uraemia, Generalised arteriosclerosis, and Arteriosclerotic dementia. These degenerative diseases illustrated just how much toll the trauma of his business career and his personal circumstances had taken on his body and mind. He died at Larkspur, Hewling Way, Worthing and the informant on his death certificate was his niece Ellen Gertrude Ashton who was married to Michael Ashton, her middle name after her grandmother.

His obituary in *"The Times"* was fulsome:

THE TIMES
August 17th 1976
Mr Frederick Miles.

"Mr Frederick George Miles FRAeS, MSAE, whose brilliance in the design and production of light aircraft was unparallelled, died on August 15th."

There followed a very detailed account of his life and career, continuing:

"Such experience made him scornful of official timidity and misjudgement, he once compiled a bitter, but amusing, list of the engineering feats officially declared to be impossible but actually achieved."

Again the word "bitter" enters the equation.

Referring to the famous court case against him the obituary goes on:

"The Old Bailey Jury stopped proceedings and threw out the case. . . . he did not allow the flow of creative ideas to be cut off. He was Chairman of F.G. Miles Ltd to 1961, he widened his technical and business activities and plunged into electronics. His work was, as in his early days, at Shoreham. He was a Freeman

of the Guild of Air Pilots and Navigators and a member of the Royal Aero Club."

We read in November of his will:

"Mr F.G. Miles of Ashurst left £192,766."

Another seven and a half years and we will see Blossom's obituary.

* * *

Blossom's increasing blindness was a concern to her; she had great faith in acupuncture and Joan Angell took her to London for regular sessions, eventually taking her to a local acupuncturist. There were rumours that a specialist in Switzerland could perform an operation to improve her sight even though it had been diagnosed as an hereditary disease of old age and therefore incurable. Dr Csato, who had played such a part in setting up the Technical School of which she was so proud and continued to be, persuaded her that there was a good chance of this operation succeeding. So she, with her sister Dinah and Joan Angell, set off for Switzerland, where she had the operation and was in hospital for a week or so while Joan and Dinah enjoyed the scenery, but of course there was absolutely no improvement. Once again she took it stoically at least outwardly, but her sight, which all her life had almost been in jeopardy, was now so minimal that she was registered blind.

It was not really in her nature to give up and she tried to continue to do things like knitting, with which she got in a frightful "wazzle," the faithful Jan and Margery Cobby having to untangle it. She liked Margery to read poetry to her and bring her her evening glass of sherry. Joan Angell didn't care for poetry herself so she read newspapers to her.

Having been such a keen gardener all her life, it was strange that after her sight deteriorated so badly she would not even go out into the garden with Joan Angell and could not be persuaded to leave the house at all. Towards the end of her life Jan became her nurse as well as all else.

Her sister Dinah was a regular visitor and the local village people had a genuine affection for her, as did David Russell and Margery Cobby; Joan Angell was often there but it was Jan Praulins who devoted himself to every physical task necessary to looking after her.

Eventually it seemed that uncharacteristically she just "gave up" and died gradually and peacefully, but she had physical ailments like F.G. that contributed to her death, the typical diseases of old age. She was able to die at Batts, which was her own house designed to her own ideas and her memories of 22 Bedford Square. Echoes of Aunt Maxine and her father, Sir Johnston, lingered in the design and ambience of that Regency building in its own secluded grounds. Her later life harked back to her early days, Woodley and Lands End House, and the frantic war years were forgotten in the leisurely village life in Ashurst. Peace at last, at long last.

EPILOGUE

In the years of her retirement, after F.G.'s death and the increasing problems with her sight, all those who knew her and looked after her stressed that in spite of her blindness she retained her serenity and her interest in life and in others.

Her devoted retainer, who had been with her for thirty-five years said that: "She was a grand old lady, and very formidable right up to her last days; we were all very fond of her." The newspapers managed to get his name wrong, calling him Jines Brulins, when his name was Jan Praulins, but it was understandable for, in spite of living in England for so many years, his accent was impenetrable; indeed in translation the spelling may be in doubt.

She died at her home, Batts, at Ashurst of some of the symptoms of old age, including a heart problem, although the doctor certified one of the causes as "Great Age"; at eighty-two, that does not seem too great an age. She died on the 6th April 1984 and the informant was Joan Angell, one of three of the Angell family who had remained so loyal throughout the tribulations of Miles Aircraft Ltd.

Her funeral and cremation at Worthing Crematorium was attended by some of her old students of Miles Aeronautical Technical School as well as her family and friends; it was a lovely spring day, the sunshine lighting up the flowers and the trees.

Little aircraft designed by her still soar up into the heavens sixty years on, and all over the world from Australia and Canada to the United States of America, from France and Germany and Israel to Scotland and Ireland, her students will never forget her, and their children and grandchildren are still benefitting from her methods of education, her inspiration and her example.

APPENDIX 1

Since the main text of this book was completed and indexed, details of Blossom's flying Log Book have been made available by courtesy of Peter Amos; these are reproduced below with his comments in italics.

FLYING RECORD OF MRS MAXINE FRANCES MARY FREEMAN-THOMAS OF WICKHAM PLACE, HURST-PIERPOINT, SUSSEX, BORN SEPTEMBER 22ND 1901.

[Maxine ("Blossom") was taught to fly by F.G. Miles at Shoreham and she made her first flight, of just 15 minutes duration, on June 2nd 1930 in the Avro 504K G-EBYB. Most of her flying training was carried out in this Avro with F.G. Miles, but on June 27th 1930 she flew with Cecil L. Pashley for the first time, also in G-EBYB. Blossom made her first solo flight in G-EBYB on July 25th 1930, after 15 hours 18 minutes dual instruction.

Many other different types of aircraft were to be flown by Maxine and these are shown below with the date of her first flight in each. In her Log there are occasional brief remarks in the "Comments" column, and these are reproduced here with an interpretation if appropriate:]

1930

17th Jun.	G-AACW	Avro 504K	
11th Jul.	G-AABF	Blackburn Bluebird III	
27th Jul.	G-ABAF	DH.60 Gipsy Moth	Fielden *[pilot?]*–Ford *[destination?]*
31st Jul.	G-AADF	Avro Avian IV	
13th Oct.	G-EBZG	DH.60X Moth	
31st Oct.	G-EBYP	Avro Avian IIIA	
30th Nov.	G-EBZG	DH.60X Moth	with L.E.R.B. (Lionel Bellairs)

1931

5th Jan.	G-AAVM	Avro Avian IVM	
15th Jan.	G-AAVD	Southern Martlet	5 minute flight
6th Feb.	G-ABIF	Southern Martlet	
16th Mar.	G-ABDO	Robinson Redwing 2	
8th Apr.	G-AAWT	Desoutter I	Shoreham–Le Bourget with F.G. Miles
22nd Apr.	G-AATF	Desoutter I	Poix–Ostend
29th Apr.	G-ABKI	Avro Sports Avian	
1st May	G-AADE	Westland Widgeon III	
17th May	G-ABJW	Southern Metal Martlet	

[By May 27th Blossom had completed 100 hrs 34 mins flying.]

18th Jun.	G-ABLB	Puss Moth
27th Jul.	G-AAII	Southern Martlet
16th Sept.	G-EBZG	DH.60X Moth

[This flight was the last Blossom made from Shoreham. F.G. Miles had emigrated to South Africa in August 1931 only to return soon afterwards. The following year they married and settled in Sevenoaks, Kent, using the local aerodrome at Penshurst for their occasional flying activities. Blossom's next recorded flight was from there on January 3rd 1932.]

1932

3rd Jan.	G-ABJS	Simmonds Spartan 3-seater	To Reading
15th Jan.	G-ABJS	Simmonds Spartan 3-seater	
31st Jan.	G-ABJS	Simmonds Spartan 3-seater	
16th Feb.	G-ABJS	Simmonds Spartan 3-seater	
20th Mar.	G-ABJS	Simmonds Spartan 3-seater	
16th May	G-AAGY	Simmonds Spartan	To Bristol and ???????*, 40 minutes return

[This place name is indecipherable in the original Log. G-AAGY was seen by myself many years later (in about 1945/6) in a terrible condition at a Country Club on Nutfield Marsh, north of Redhill Aerodrome, having been in open storage with the wings folded since the outbreak of war. It was scrapped in 1947.]*

25th May	G-AADF	Avro Avian IV	To Yate

[This was the last flight Blossom made from Penshurst. She did not fly again until 1933, and all her subsequent flights were from Woodley.]

1933

13th Feb.	G-EBUS	DH.60X Moth	To Reading with F.G. Miles
30th Mar.	?	Miles Hawk	5 minutes solo
3th Apr.	?	Miles Hawk	5 minutes with F.G. Miles
3rd Apr.	?	Miles Hawk	10 minutes solo
5th Apr.	G-ACAS	Fairey Fox I	With F.G. Miles
11th Apr.	?	Miles Hawk	2 flights
15th Apr.	G-ACDI	Tiger Moth	
16th Apr.	G-ACGH	Miles Hawk	15 minutes with F.G. Miles
12th Sep.	G-ACJY	Miles Hawk	10 minutes at Cannes
7th Nov.	G-ACLB	Miles Hawk	

1934

21st Mar.	?	Miles Hawk 'Gypsy'	
21st Mar.	G-ACNW	Miles Hawk	
22nd Mar.	G-ACNW	Miles Hawk	
17th Jul.	?	Miles Hawk	5 minutes–experimental flaps
2nd Aug.	G-ACVM	Miles Hawk	Gipsy Major

[This was actually a M.2F Hawk Major.]

1935

4th Nov.	G-ADLC	Miles M.3B Falcon Six	Farnborough – Reading
24th Nov.	G-ADWT	Miles M.2W Hawk Trainer	With F.G. Miles
24th Nov.	G-ADWV	Miles M.2W Hawk Trainer	With F.G. Miles
24th Nov.	G-ADWU	Miles M.2W Hawk Trainer	With F.G. Miles
4th Dec.	U1(?)	Miles M.7 Nightkawk	Two flights with F.G. Miles
11th Dec.	G-ADXA	Miles M.7 Nighthawk	With F.G. Miles

[This was the last flight to be recorded in Blossom's Log Book.]

APPENDIX 2

The following two extracts from prewar editions of *"The Aeroplane"* magazine are reproduced here by courtesy of *"Aeroplane Monthly"*; they give some detailed insight as to Blossom's duties as a C.A.G. Commissioner.

SEPTEMBER 28TH, 1938

WOMEN'S DAY AT CHIGWELL

Chigwell's new aeroplane for Civil Air Guards, to be administered by the Romford Flying Club and by the National Women's Air Reserve, was opened with due ceremony by Mrs F.G. Miles, Civil Air Guard Commissioner, on Sept. 24. Chigwell is to be used as an instructional aerodrome for Cags until Fairlop, which is close by, is in running order. Presumably some new site will then have to be found, to prevent Cags from embroiling themselves with regular air services in the prevailing fog.

. . . Mr and Mrs Miles arrived exactly at 14.30 hrs in their Miles Monarch (130 hp Gipsy Major). Mrs Miles declared the aerodrome open, fulfilling her first public duty as a Cag Commissioner. She inspected a Guard of Honour on the National Women's Air Reserve under Mrs Gabrielle Patterson.

NOVEMBER 16TH, 1938

LIGHT ON THE C.A.G.

Mrs F.G. Miles, Commissioner of the Civil Air Guard, addressing the Women's Engineering Society on Nov. 8 on the Civil Air Guard, said that the C.A.G. was organised hurriedly, but she was surprised at the surprise of the Air Ministry at the response. Those in aviation knew well what the demand was. Events had been hard on the flying clubs and the Air Ministry wanted to help them

Mrs Miles, explaining the C.A.G., said that the Commissioners soon found that 95% of the clubs could not train all their applicants within four years, and some might take ten. So the lists were closed, but applications are still received by C.A.G. Headquarters, who are trying to distribute them.

The Commissioners had suggested lectures to mass meetings of the C.A.G. to overcome the ignorance of many recruits. The Air Ministry said that a scheme of their own was in hand and might be ready in December.

Mrs Miles was sorry she had not a sample uniform. It had been chosen for appearance, price and wear. She had sent overalls to the laundry, to be treated as her sheets were treated. The overalls stood the test the better.

She had already visited about half the clubs in her area – the south of England. Almost all the instructors had reported well of their pupils. Pupils without ability could be abandoned after six hours, and the club would get compensation from the Government. The estimate was that about 20% would thus be lost, but the figure so far was about 5%. The Commissioners hope to arrange advanced training for particularly good Cags, and also training after the 'A' licence.

In reply to questions Mrs Miles said that 50% of applicants were under 30 years of age; she had no idea how the Air Ministry meant to employ women Cags in the event of war; and no scheme existed for the training of ground engineers under the C.A.G.

Miss Amy Johnson thought lighter aeroplanes would be needed and at a reasonable price. Cags of special ability should get further training at low rates. The Royal Aero Club should not be allowed to charge one guinea on every licence. [This is the fee for the R.Ae.C. Certificate, which is not part of the licence. – ED.] Cheap rates for mid-week flying helped those who least needed it, those who had least money could usually fly only at weekends.

Mrs Richard Pearse (formerly Miss Dorothy Spicer) said that in selecting Mrs Miles the Powers-That-Be showed unusual intelligence. She was a "designing woman," a born mathematician, quite at home with X and Y and squared paper, and she ought to understand the problems of the C.A.G. very well.

INDEX